'O' IS FIR INGIN

ALSO BY MAE STEWART

Dae Yeh Mind Thon Time?

'O' IS FIR INGIN

MAE STEWART

BLACK & WHITE PUBLISHING

First published 2010
by Black & White Publishing Ltd
29 Ocean Drive, Edinburgh EH6 6JL

1 3 5 7 9 10 8 6 4 2   10 11 12 13

ISBN: 978 1 84502 308 9

Typeset by Iolaire Typesetting, Newtonmore
Printed and bound in the UK by J F Print Ltd., Sparkford

CONTENTS

For 'Wee Mary' with love always,
Mamie

INTRODUCTION

These reminiscences are a compilation of my own personal memories of my life, in my home town of Dundee, from the mid-1940s to the 1970s, and onwards.

For those of you who are joining me for the first time; welcome. In the last sixty years, modern technology has taken us to where only Dan Dare or Flash Gordon went when I was a kid. The television has replaced the old battery-powered radios that were part of my first entertainment. The computer has given us access to the whole world. Back then, we only had access to the streets and the town that surrounded us!

But some things never change. And some things surpass dialects, decades and technology of any kind. Kids still like to hear what it was like: 'Lang afore yeh were boarn!' I know I did when I was wee.

Mums and dads, grannies and granddads just love telling: 'Whit it wiz like when I wiz your age.'

So join me as we roll back the years. Join in some of the old Dundee Street songs and games that you thought you'd forgotten. Go back in your mind's eye to some of the places you worked in that are now just a memory of the past!

As we travel along, I'm sure you'll say, 'Eh remember that!'

Some of you who are decades younger than me (lucky you) will say; 'Whit dae yeh mean nae computers, nae television, nae mobiles, no even any hot water? How did yeh manage?'

Well . . . we did!

Bon Voyage!

Mae Stewart

1

ME, JEEMIE AN MILL RAILINS

I was born in the attic of a tenement, in a street called Watt Street, which was off the Hawkhill, up the West End of Dundee, on an April Morning in 1940. I spent the first year of my life there before I moved just streets away to a two-roomed (14 feet by 12 feet) ground-floor flat with an outside toilet up the adjoining close.

This cul-de-sac was called the 'Warkie Roadie' (Work Road) and was to be my home for the first nine years of my life. There would be seven of us living in these two rooms before we eventually became eligible for our 'new hoose'.

The Warkie Roadie housed a five-storey tenement, including the attics. The tenements were on one side of the cul-de-sac and the mill was on the other. There were only two closes (entrances) in the actual cul-de-sac and an outside staircase that ran along the back of the buildings and gave access to some of the other houses that adjoined our tenements.

The huge mill stack, which must have belched forth smoke every day, was just yards away from my door, but I can't remember even noticing it when I was a kid.

The entrance to the mill was from Annfield Road,

1

at the end of the cul-de-sac. I can remember waking up and hearing folk running along the street after the mill 'bummer' (siren) had summoned them to their work. The siren sounded just like the ones that you heard in the war movies when there was an air raid.

But before the siren, I was sometimes wakened up by the 'chapper-upper'; our human alarm clock. Beat that with your electronic clock-radio that wakes you up with your favourite song. I was never Mrs Sunshine in the mornings and I think I'd have murdered a clock that woke me up by singing merrily to me!

Anyway ... the chapper-upper's job was to go round folks houses early in the morning and get them up for their work by knocking on the window, then banging on it if you didn't answer him. I think there was a rule that he only knocked three times (maybe that's where they got the song from) and then you'd had it, for he'd more than you to get up in time for their work!

He'd rap gently on the window: 'Are Yeh Up?' No answer.
He'd knock a bit louder: 'Are Yeh Up?' No answer.
He'd batter on the window: *'Are yeh up?'*
At Last . . . 'Eh! Eh'm up!'

To someone listening in, who came from some far off place like Edinburgh, this might have sounded like a secret code sequence of some kind, because the early morning reveilles that I remember hearing went something like this:

'Y-up? . . . y-up? . . . y-up? . . . m-up!'

And this poor guy had to do this for as many houses as paid him.

I wonder who got him up for his work? Actually it *was* known for the chapper-upper to sleep in on occasions, and then the whole 'get-up-fir-yehr-work' routine went pear-shaped. I bet he was popular on that day, with everybody getting money knocked off their wages because they were late.

Sometime, when the bummer had woken me, I would count the times it droned on until I could get back to sleep. It would sound three times. The first time was at about 6.45 a.m. I think, which gave the workers fifteen minutes to get cracking and get in on time. So I guess it sounded for about two minutes and then was off for three minutes, and it did this three times, *every* morning.

Between that, the noise of the mills and the rest of the inhabitants of our cul-de-sac, no wonder I could sleep through an invasion now!

At lunchtime this bummer would start the same palaver all over again to tell folk it was time to go and have something to eat. Then it would do the same to get them back into work. We called lunchtime 'dinner time' when I was a kid, and dinner time was called 'tea time.' Only posh folk had 'lunch!'

I bet the only sound that everybody who worked in that mill really welcomed was the five o'clock bummer that released them at the end of the day. That's when the workers would come teeming out through that mill gate.

If you were around at lunchtime, you always knew when it was time for the workers to get out, because the lodge keeper would open up the gates, and if you looked towards the big mill doors you would see the workers gathered there, ready for the off!

Or alternatively you could watch for my grannie's cat whose name was Jeemie.

When you saw Jeemie appearing at the mill gate, you knew it was almost 'Dehve-oot-the-door time'. The reason for the rush was that workers back then only had thirty minutes to get home, get some food, and then back again.

My maternal grandmother lived next door to me and worked in the mill. I can remember, when the schools were off, going up to the mill gate to wait for her coming home for 'lunch', and the Charge of the Light Brigade had nothing on our mill workers when that bummer sounded twelve o'clock.

I used to think it was like the mêlée coming out of the Saturday Cinema Club, only adults instead of kids. But they didn't have to slap their thighs to spur on their kiddy-on horses; they were faster than any real horses!

Well! I became famous one lunchtime when I was standing outside waiting for my grannie. I was with my older brother and we were leaning on the railings waiting for the noon bummer to sound, when we were joined on grannie-watch by Jeemie.

The railings were about five to six feet high and ran alongside the main entrance to the mill. To this day, and for reasons known only to the God of kids, I decided to see if I could stick my head through the railings and then pull it back out . . . just to see if I could.

My brother's half-hearted warning of, 'Yeh'd maybe better no?' went unheeded, mainly because I think he wanted to see if I could do this 'feat' as well and, after all, it wasn't his head!

So I did indeed just shove, and jiggle, until my head went right through the railings.

Well, my ears went through flat since they were being pushed sideways onto the sides of my head, but then they just jumped back to their normal shape! If you've ever tried to pull your head backerties ('backwards' to folk who had 'lunch' back then), from between two solid iron railings, with your ears getting pushed in the opposite direction from how they would normal sit, then I can tell you first-hand . . . It hurts!

I was well and truly *stuck!*

We manoeuvred and we re-jiggled, while I kept shouting; 'Get me oot! Eh'm stuck! oowww! Yehr haulin meh ears aff! Eh'm stuck!'

My brother yelled; 'Yeh wee numpty. Eh telt yeh!' Because he could see quite clearly the gathering storm.

Then the lunchtime bummer and I went *off* in tandem!

I started screeching at the top of my voice, as the descending hoard came running out the door. Well that stopped them in their tracks!

The lodge keeper came flying out off his hut just inside the work gates, to see what the stramash at the railings was. I bet he didn't think a wee kid could outshine the mill bummer!

My grannie dashed over and looked like she couldn't believe it. She even ignored Jeemie, who was twining himself round her legs in the hope that she'd hurry up and get home to give him his dinner.

The assembled body tried to get me out. Instructions were issued by those who thought they were expert in dealing with heids stuck in railings.

'Watch ehr heid!' and 'Mind no puhl too hard on ehr ears.' That got my vote! This was all accompanied to my weeping and wailing. Could they shift 'meh heid?' — No, they could not!

By this time I was like a street show for the rest of the workers as they hurried past the wee crowd gathered around me.

My brother had run for my mother, who appeared like a whippet and never even yelled at me, and this made me worse as I knew I was in real trouble then!

So then somebody ran to get the fire brigade!

The fire brigade duly arrived, surveyed the scene and went to work.

They prised the railings open a wee bit with what looked like big pliers to me. They put a towel round my neck and one over my head. Then one fireman held onto me, while the other two got their giant pliers and really heaved at that railing, bent it to 'wee heid shape', pulled gently and, hey presto . . . glorious freedom!

I was escorted home by one of the firemen, my mother, my brother, my grannie and Jeemie the cat.

My grannie now had about two minutes to gulp a cup of tea, feed the cat, wash her face and then dash back to work, so she vanished pronto!

The fireman stayed with us for a wee while, saying to me:

'Move yehr heid tae the side, slowly. Nod up an doon, slowly! Follow meh finger!" And he waved his finger back and forth in front of my eyes. 'Na! You'll dae! Yeh'll be fine. It's only red, an that'll die doon!'

So he exited stage right as well!

My mother examined my red neck and ears for about the hundredth time, all the while saying:

'Dinna you move fae that chair, an jist sit still. Dae yeh ken whit? You twa's gonna be the death o' me yet! An then whit'll yeh dae, weh naebody tae bale yeh oot o' a yehr shenanegins?'

Yup! I was definitely getting better!

When I think on this now, nobody even thought about sending for an ambulance or anything! Talk about just getting on with it!

Anyway, I knew I was much better when my ears stopped throbbing. But then they started getting another verbal battering from my mother when I said they felt much better:

Much guid lugs dae you, fir yeh niver listen tae a word
Eh say tae yeh anyway! An you're as much tae blame.'
Says she pointing at my brother; 'You should've been
lookin efter ehr, an no lettin ehr dae a daft caper like
stickin ehr heid through the railins.

My brother and I just looked at each other. I guess we
figured life was back to normal. And anyway I still had my
ears stuck to the side of my head. Things could have been
much worse.

And so that day moved on, but my fame remained for a
wee while, as the railing stayed bent out of shape forever.

I remember soon after the 'There's the bairn that stuck
ehr hied through the mill railins' episode, going back up to
the work gate to wait for my grannie, and this man passing
said to me:

'Hey is that no a coincidence? There's a railin that's the
same shape as your heid.'

Now, let me tell you about Jeemie, my grannie's cat, who
was also famous at the mill railings in his own right.

Jeemie used to go up to the mill gate every day to wait for
my grannie coming out of her work. He appeared at about
five minutes to twelve and waited for her, went home for
something to eat, vanished and then went back to meet her
at knocking-off time, when he would appear at five minutes
to five each night and wait for her once again.

That cat could be anywhere at all in Dundee and would
still appear sauntering up the road *every* day at these
specific times.

All the kids where I lived knew him and if they were up
at the mill gates, just beside the railings, when he appeared,
they would speak to him.

But here's the real spooky thing. That cat never ever went up to the mill gate on Saturday or Sunday. Even if my grannie wasn't in the house and he was out and about, he still never went near that mill at the weekend. Must've been a working-class cat right enough!

Folk used to say you could have set your clock by that cat. And so you could! How clever was he?

The mill and the mill railings are long gone. Only ghosts hang around the huge listed chimney stack that, to this day, marks my first world. You'd never guess that any of us were ever there at all.

Jeemie's long gone too.

But memories are wonderful things! Memories can go on forever!

And I remember yet when Jeemie and I were both famous, up at the mill gate railings that were just round the corner from the Warkie Roadie.

2

FUN AN GEMES FAE THE WARKIE ROADIE

When I was a kid the cindered cul-de-sac and the streets around me were my playground. And if we weren't away down to the 'Meddlie' (Magdelen Yard park area beside the Tay) with my mother, then we had to make our own entertainment.

We had the usual board games, jigsaws, toys . . . but most of the games we played were conjured up from our imagination and, of course, cost very little. One of my earliest games was called 'Fleg the Neebours'.

This was masterminded by my older brother, for when we were fed up playing 'normal' stuff and we felt really brave. Then we had a game of 'Fleg the Neebours'. That was until we were reported back to headquarters and then it was us that got the fleg!

We used to 'borrow' one of the Silver Cross prams that were all the go in these days. These were huge posh baby carriages with chrome bits all over them and were passed round numerous infants, related or otherwise, and held an avalanche of washing when they were relegated to 'washie tannies' (Public Washing House 'perambulators' if you lived somewhere posh!)

My brother would ask one of our neighbours if he could borrow the pram to walk about with 'the bairn' to help my mother out. If they consented then we were on our way.

He would hoist me into the pram and stuff me into the space that was meant for an infant, then he'd pull up the waterproof cover that covered half the opening of the pram hood and we'd go off marching up and down the street. Not our street, of course, somebody else's!

My job was to stay as quiet as possible (there was a challenge in itself), and then when some woman passing by stopped us and asked him, 'Is that you oot shoagin (gently shaking) the bairn tae get him tae sleep fir yehr mither?' he would nod innocently.

If they fell for it, they might say, 'How's the wee ane getting on anyway?' Then stick their head into the pram, to be confronted by this gigantic 'bairn' that was me, taking up the whole pram, who just sat and smiled at them.

Most women just laughed and walked away. But if the woman who'd looked in the pram had no sense of humour (in our opinion), she'd stomp off with a:

'Well, Eh hope you twa find it funny when Eh tell yehr mither!'

That's when we hurriedly dumped the pram back to its owner and waited to see what was going to happen, or if we'd got away with it. Talk about living in hope!

We knew it was reckoning time when my mother would yell from the door step:

'Hoi! You twa! Get alang here. Eh want tae speak tae you.'

Oh! She of forked tongue! Speaking was the least of it!

* * *

My older brother was my hero when I was a kid and he liked nothing better than an adventure out of the ordinary, no matter how much trouble it got him into. I followed him around like a collie dug, and marched right into trouble with him! My older sister tells this story about him when she was about eight and he was about five.

My mother had taken the two of them for the 'Sunday Visits' to my paternal grandparents who lived in Byron Street and my Great-Auntie Mary who lived in Hill Street. Both houses were adjacent to the Law Hill.

Auntie Mary had a budgie called Joey (what else) that my brother was very fond of. However, this Sunday, when they both ran through the door and he dived 'ben-the-room' to see Joey, the cage was empty, because poor Joey had died that morning!

My brother got really upset about this and as 'upset' was not his usual style, my Auntie Mary decided that they would go and give Joey a funeral up at my grandparents hen run on the Law Hill.

So that's what they did. She wrapped Joey up in tissue paper and the four of them trotted over to the hen run with my brother carrying Joey. They were met there by my grandparents, who were informed about poor Joey and asked if they could give him a send off by burying him at the hen run.

No Problem!

They all set about preparing for the burial. My grandmother dug a special wee grave beside some of her flowers, under one of the bushes, and they all gathered round to see Joey laid to rest. Then she said:

'Eh think weh should say a prayer fir Joey.'

So the wee group of mourners stood silently as my grandmother said her prayer for the budgie. Then she turned to my brother:

'There diz that no make yeh feel better, son?'

He looked round the group:

Eh that wiz great, Granny! Eh enjoyed that! Dae yeh think weh could maybe dig him up an dae it a ower agen?

But back to the Warkie Roadie!

A regular occasion in my neck of the woods was women having babies, which provided us with a game of chance!

When you had a 'new bairn' and if it was to be christened, it was compulsory to make up a 'Christening piece'. This was a wee paper bag that contained a 'piece' (sandwich), an apple or an orange. A biscuit and, sometimes, money that ranged from a copper or two up to the huge sum of a shilling.

If the baby was a boy, it was the first wee lassie you met when you came out of the close that Sunday that got the Christening Piece, and vice versa if it was a girl.

So if someone that lived nearby had a baby boy, I was up with the lark that Sunday, and playing nonchalantly about the close in the hope that the christening party wouldn't bump into anyone else before they spotted me. I collected quite a few christening pieces in my time.

* * *

I loved 'boxies' (Hop Scotch). When I think about this game I recall that we used to draw out the squares, we would be hopping in and out of, on the pavement, then number them, get an old boot polish tin for throwing up into the square, try to leap to where the tin landed, and then hop all the way back down the boxie. Or you'd draw a huge continuous circle starting from the inside and working out, mark out sections, number them and that made a different game!

Our pavements must have been continuously covered in

chalk boxies and pavement artistry, but folk never seemed to mind that.

* * *

'Jumpin ower the Devil's Cracks' was a street game you could play anywhere. You just had to walk along the street from A to B, and never walk on the splits between the paving stones, or cracks on the paving stones. Never mind the folk that you bumped into because your head was down looking for cracks in the pavement. If there were a few of you playing that added to the fun no end.

I loved to play at pretend Shops. I'd borrow some of my mother's tinned stuff, some vegetables and other small household items, and then I'd line up my wares on the pavement like soldiers.

I had a couple of soup spoons that I pretended were butter skelpers (small wooden paddles used by shopkeepers to cut a lump of butter out of the butter barrel and mould it into a square), and made up some 'Slappy-Gutters' (earth and water, slapped around the basin, preferably with bare hands, resulting in a Class A Slappy-Gutters). Then you just kept slapping away until you had a nice batch of kiddie-on butter! As you can imagine, making the butter was one of the best bits, and since all of this was outdoors in front of my own house, I could mess away to my heart's content.

Then my mother would just appear with a basin of warm water and soap, wash me, slosh the pavement with the rest of the soapy water and, hey presto, that was the 'Dairy' all cleaned up!

I had a wee cash register to keep my 'money' in. Now here's the thing! 'Money' to play with back then used to be bits of old china. If it was a big piece of broken china

with a gold bit on it that was the big money. Then it graduated down to just a small piece of plain white plate or such
like.

I used to swap china pieces with my girl pals and you
used to have to give a lot of plain plate to get a wee bit china
cup with gold round the rim in return.

* * *

We saved up scraps and swapped them. We played a game
where you scattered your scraps in pages throughout a
book, then each took a turn in opening up a page and, if the
scrap was there, it was yours. I just loved Crinoline Ladies
and Angel scraps, and had them in all sizes. I've seen scraps
in the shops not too long ago, so I guess wee lassies still
save up scraps.

* * *

I have to admit that as a kid anything that made me sit
down for more than ten minutes instantly lost its appeal for
me. I was more into the 'dehvin aboot like a forkie gemes'
as my mother would have said if you'd asked her. I blame
it on the fact that I was 'in between' two brothers and had
an older brother who thought he was Errol Flynn *and* Dan
Dare all rolled into one!

This next game I loved was unisex and it was called
'pinner'.

We had these two by two inch pieces of lead made at
the boatyard. You laid a spare pinner against the side of
pavement kerb. Everybody would throw their own pinner
at it, and the one that hit it was bulls-eye. Then you all got
points depending how near you were to the target pinner.

I loved to play 'Fehve Stanes'. You picked up five small
stones, lay four of the stones across the back of your

knuckles with your hand facing downwards and placed the other one further up your hand. The aim was to throw the stones up in the air as far as you could, and then try to catch all five stones as they fell to the ground. Points were allotted by counting the stones you caught. I was a dab hand at that game.

Oh! And one of my very favourites was to stick a tennis ball in one of my mother's old nylon stockings and play 'Stottin-Ba'.

You took the ball and shoved it right down to the toe of the stocking, and then tied a knot in the stocking to keep it in place. Then you found the nearest wall, in my case across the road at the mill wall if it was fair, and inside the close that ran alongside my house if it was raining.

My constant warning from my mother if I was going to play inside the close was: 'Mind an no bang that ba' up against next door's closie wa'. Jist mak a noise on yehr ain wa.'

The fact that the close was about two-feet wide meant the neighbours would have had to have been deaf not to hear the noise, but at least they were spared the banging. I bet there were some days when it was raining that the folk who lived up closes wished they were a nomadic tribe in the middle of the Sahara!

My mother always examined the stocking before I went out. She'd say:

'Let me look that yehr no takin ane that's too new or that Eh kin darn.'

Yes, they did have to darn their nylon stockings in these days! None of your, 'Och! Eh've got a ladder in meh tights,' then just binning them and going to the drawer for a new pair.

In fact, I hated it when my mother darned either the

soles or the heels of my thick winter stockings when I was a kid. Only my Auntie Mary could darn so that it was as smooth as when they were new, so she usually did all the darning for us. My mother, on the other hand, who always did everything at a mile a minute, just darned them any old how, and you'd just to put up with the lumpy bits jagging your feet!

I'd have to say here that I always hated these winter stockings with a vengeance anyway. If I was made to wear them, I would pick away at the knee until there was a wee hole, and then I'd skid along the pavement and tear them properly. So I never had many stockings that needed darned, as you couldn't darn a hole the size of a football!

My mother would accuse me:

'Yeh've deliberately ripped they stockin's, hivn't yeh?'

I would plead pathetically, without even a blush:

'Eh canna help it if Eh fa' when Eh'm runnin! She'd reply:

'Do Eh look like Eh came up the Tey (River Tay) in a banana boat?'

I think I just shut up then, and quit when I was ahead and not getting shoved or shaken like a rabbit!

Anyway, back to playing 'Stottin-Ba'.

I'd twist the top of the old stocking round my hand, stand with my back against the wall, then swing the stocking and ball up and down, up and down. With the stocking being stretchy, the harder I swung, the further it went, and the more of an impact and bounce it had.

So there I'd be walloping away good style; first to my right side, then to my left side, above my head, over one shoulder, over the next shoulder. I'd swing one leg to the side and bounce the ball between my legs, swing the other leg, do a jack-knife leap and bounce it between both legs. The jack-knife 'leapie-up' was the most difficult for me, and half the time I ended up losing my balance, conking myself on the heid, or nearly putting my eye out.

There were special songs that someone back in the dark ages had made up to go with all these ball aerobics. So while all this *ba-bump ba-bump ba-bump ba-bump* was going on against the wall, I was jumping about like a forkie *and* belting out 'Ba-Sangs' at the top of my voice in time with the *ba-bumping.*

Here are four of my favourite 'Ba-Sangs':

> *Meh lads a corker*
> *Heez a New Yorker*
> *He behs me everythin tae keep me in style*
> *Eh've got a pair o' hips*
> *Jist like twa battleships*
> *An that's whyyy he loooovees*
> *me-eeeee so-hooooooooooooooo!*

> *Stot Stot — Ba Ba*
> *Forty lassies on the la*
> *No a lad amongst them a'*
> *Stot Stot — Ba Ba.*

> *PK chewin gum, penny fir a packit*
> *Furst yeh chew it, then yeh crack it*
> *Then yeh stick it on yehr jaicket*
> *PK chewin gum, penny fir a packit.*

And, finally, one of my very favourites.

> *One . . . two . . . three . . . O'Leerie*
> *Eh saw Wahllice Beerie*
> *Sittin on eez bumbaleerie*
> *Eatin' chocolate soldiers.*

Do you know there's just so much information in these wee street songs about the times we lived in? The influence of American music. Wallace Beerie was a famous film star and you did get wee chocolate soldiers wrapped in gold or silver paper.

I would keep repeating these songs over and over, until my arms got tired or I'd walloped my head, legs, arms and ankles, or fallen over enough times that I'd to have a break.

Or I wore a hole in the stocking with all the walloping off the wall and the ball bounced out and crowned some poor kid I was playing with at the time. Or, and this was more to the point, my Mother or one of the neighbours threatened to do me a damage if:

'Eh battered that wa' weh that ba' any mair, an sung ane o' they bliddy sangs one mair time.'

Can you imagine the *ba-bumping* that went on if there were two or more wee lassies playing up the same close? It must have been like having a giant pinball machine attached to the wall of the building. Folk back then must have been saints right enough!

* * *

Anyway I thought I'd translate these four children's' street songs into English, for the benefit of those amongst us who haven't heard them before and are not bi-lingual:

> *My boyfriend's very special*
> *He comes from New York*
> *He buys me loads of stylish up-to-date clothing*
> *I'm not a lady of small stature*
> *But my boyfriend prefers me as I am and*
> *   that's why he's in love with me.*

Bounce Bounce — Ball Ball
Forty Girls up at the Law Hill
Not a boy in sight
Bounce Bounce — Ball Ball.

PK chewing gum, one pence per packet
First you chew it, then you blow it through
     your teeth and make cracking noises.
Then if you want to save your chewing gum for
     later on, adhere it to the underside of the lapel
     of your jacket.
PK chewing gum, one pence per packet.

One . . . two . . . three . . .O'Leerie
I spied that well-renowned film star Mr Wallace
     Beerie
Sitting on his derriere
Digesting chocolate soldiers.

Yup! You're dead right! It absolutely loses all its fun and magic in the translation. And anyway I can't see anyone that 'adhered' anything sticking a bit 'Chewnie' to their jacket and saving it for later on!

* * *

Back then it was common practice for kids to share chewing gum that someone else was already chewing away on. They would either offer you a bit, 'Dae yeh want a buhttie chewnie?' or by request: 'Geez a buht o' yehr chewnie.'

The same with an apple or a pear. Kids used to ask you; 'Kin Eh get yehr catties?' I have no idea where the word 'cattie' comes from, but it means 'what you are not going to eat', which in most cases was biscuit/cake crumbs, only the core if it was an apple and the stalk if it was a pear. So 'catties' wouldn't even have fed Oliver Twist!

I was *never* into any of this mouth-to-mouth sharing even as a kid. I blame that on a father that just about had a fit if you sniffed when he was eating a meal, never mind caught you eating something that somebody else had already put in their mouth.

He used to say to us:

'If Eh catch you eatin anything oot o' somebody else's mooth, then yehr fir it.' We never needed an explanation of what 'it' was. We knew first-hand that 'it' was to be avoided at all costs.

My mother, on the other hand, was never scared of giving her kids nightmares, and would say to us:

'Dae yeh ken yeh kid get a scabby mooth, or some ither affy diseases, if yeh eat somethin' that somebody else hiz already hid in thir mooth.'

No pressure there then mother!

* * *

Another game (well more like an event) I loved when I lived in the Warkie Roadie was Guy Fawkes Night, known to us as Bonie (Bonfire) Night. In Dundee back then, lots of streets had their own bonfires, set of 'squeebs' (fireworks) and held their own street celebrations.

After teatime on Bonfire Night, the adults would make a bonfire heap using old furniture, firewood and any other old rubbish that would burn.

Bear in mind that this cul-de-sac was about twenty to thirty feet wide, and about six times that in length. The tenements were at one side of the cul-de-sac and were five storeys high, and the mill wall was at the other side.

Some of the tenements where I lived had front lands and

also back lands. A few of them had middle lands as well. That meant two or three rows of tenements all lined up behind each other.

Actually, I wish now I had a head count of how many people lived in the half mile that was my world when I was a small kid. Most of the tenements were three to five storeys high and consisted of mainly two-roomed flats that housed at least one, and in the main, four to ten/twelve people. Yes! We did know folk that had up to twelve kids in two rooms! And back in my grandmother's time that was not in the least unusual. We never got our new house in Fintry until there were *seven* of us under the one roof! Talk about herring in a barrel!

So to get back to the bonfire . . . again!

No wonder the fire brigades were kept busy on Bonfire Nights! It's a wonder we didn't have more 'Bonie Night' disasters than we did!

Once it was dark we would all gather round this huge fire. I have no recollection of a guy or anything stuck on the top, but some of the kids used to make up guys and put them in their pilers and go about asking for a penny for the guy, but according to my father:

'Weh'll hae nane o' that! That's beggin'!'

So it was 'not-now not-ever' from the boss of us.

The bonfire would be lit and everybody would cheer. When it sparked and really got going the adults would shove potatoes and chestnuts under the bottom of the fire with sticks. When they were ready we'd get them served up in a bit newspaper.

In some cases 'ready' meant 'as black as the Earl o' Hell's weistcoat' to quote my granny, but we devoured everything nonetheless!

Sometime into the proceedings us kids would be ushered

to safety before the fireworks were set off, which was down at the end of the street and away from the 'Bonie'.

My mother would drag us away like it was a spaceship that was about to be launched:

'Mind! Stey oot the road, an jist watch fae here. Yehr no wantin yehr hair burnt aff! Or anything else fir that metter! '

I told you my mother was into the scare tactics if they worked. And they usually did! None of this: ''Please be careful or you might hurt yourself, darling,' from my mother!

Finally, towards the end of the evening, somebody would collect money and go for a couple of handbasins of chips to the chip shop round the corner. These piles of chips would appear and everybody just got stuck in, or put some in a bit newspaper.

To this day I love eating chips outside, or better still a fish supper, especially when it's in the cold weather. There is definitely something really satisfying about chippers' chips or a fish supper eaten out the paper; like a fish supper hug!

Do you know what? We recycled newspapers and no mistake: they were read first; then they were put down on newly washed floors to save the dirty feet; they made 'spills' for lighting the gas cooker; they were rolled into wee bundles to act as firelighters to put beneath the coal when you were building up a fire; cut up into wee squares for toilet paper for those who couldn't afford the real thing; in some cases, they covered school jotters, (but we always used wallpaper in my house); they were put down when the sweep came; they were used for cleaning the windows with vinegar and then rubbing them shiny with another bit newspaper; for stuffing your shoes when they got soaking wet; for lining cat boxes; making sailor/pirate hats. And Och! I suppose lots other things that you remember yourselves if you're as ancient as me!

Eventually, when the bonfire started dying down, it

was doused with water, then left to just burn out overnight.

On Bonfire Night you could hear the sound of fire engines all over the place, and all through the night, as some fires just got out of hand.

Next morning some of the adults just cleared away all the debris and another 'Bonie Night' bit the dust!

* * *

Speaking of fire engines just brought this to mind. I remember when I lived in the tenements and folk who couldn't afford (or be bothered) to get their chimney swept just 'pit thir lum up'.

When the soot had gathered so much in the chimney wall, that it was falling down into their fireside grate, 'pittin thir lum up' meant getting a handful of old newspapers and making them into torches (there's something else we used newspapers for), setting them alight, then stuffing them up the chimney so all the soot caught fire. Just like a mini-mill fire, but inside a chimney.

These tenements had communal chimneys, and I can remember as a kid hearing the roar that went round the building as the whole chimney went up, and my father saying:

'Some buggar's pit newspaper up the lum agen.'

And then burnt bits of soot would begin to fall into our fireside grate.

The chimney sweep really did look like the guy from *Mary Poppins*. He'd come into the house and lay a load of old newspapers down round about the fireplace. Then he attached a huge black sheet (made of jute or ships canvas) to the mantelpiece, made sure it was all securely tucked in round about, then just shove the big long sweeper's brush with its twirly brush head round the corner of the sheet and up the chimney as far as it would go, and just keep shoving and twirling until he got most of the soot down. Then he'd call to his pal who was on the roof!

I can remember watching as the fine soot floated through the canvas and settled in the room and thinking what a marvellous job the 'Lummie Man' had, as he could get as dirty as he liked and nobody ever 'got on' to him, for that was what he did! *And . . .* he got paid money for it!

In my mind, I can hear the sweep shouting up the 'lum' to let his pal know which house he was in. They would shout 'WHOOOOOOOP-WHOOOOOOOPY' up and down the chimney to each other, until they fathomed which part of the chimney it was. Then his pal would throw another brush, tied to a rope, down the chimney. There would be a great WHOOOSH! and a pile of soot landed on the sheet.

My mother was standing by on clean-up alert as though the soot was a forerunner to the plague arriving in our house.

Immediately the sweep left, she would brush everything down at least twice — 'Tae stop the stoor fae stickin' — then get the big brush and sweep it all out the door. Then she would sweep the pavement, come back inside and get cracking with the bucket, cloth and soapy water. That's when I departed, for anything that wasn't moving was due for a good old scrub down after the sweep left!

No one panicked when a 'lum went up' unless the roaring got louder and louder, and was accompanied by a series of crackling noises that meant the bricks were splitting. Then somebody in the tenement would run to one of the shops to phone the fire brigade.

It never took the fire brigade long to reach you anyway, because everything was so near at hand, but it was impossible for them to find out who the culprit was that had started the fire.

Considering that the chimney sweep was only about one shilling and sixpence, I guess whoever 'set the lum up' must have been skint right enough!

Here's a poem/song about a 'Lum.' So for those of you who remember the tune, just pretend you're back in your own cinema club, and follow the invisible bouncing ball that's now appeared in your head:

> Oh! Dear me, meh granny's caught a flea,
> She sahted it an peppered it, an eht it fir ehr tea.
> She didna like it, so she gave it tae ehr son,
> Ehr son didna like it, so ee threw it up the lum.
> The hoose gave a shak, an the lum gave a crack,
> An doon came granny weh ehr shirt a' black.

Now, I hope you've been singing along as you made your way through this chapter. And for those of you who aren't old enough to remember these songs, ask your mother or your granny, buy/borrow a tennis ball, find yourself a wall *(not mine)*; and, hey presto. Never mind your fancy 'keep fit' games attached to your television, here's a whole new way to exercise.

* * *

At Halloween we would duck for apples, and my mother would tie a load of pancakes with jam onto a rope she'd swung from the pulley in the kitchen, and we'd to jump up and down and try to get a bite of the pancake, and in the process, of course, get covered in jam. Then we'd eat the pancakes, no matter what state they finished up in!

I would get dressed up for going 'oot gezzen' (trick or treating). We only got to visit the nearby houses, and it was compulsory that you 'did a turn', but that suited me fine.

As a kid I would have sung and danced for the world and his wife for free, never mind get somebody to pay me!

I had a wee blue, baby grand piano about twelve inches in size that I remember carrying around with me one time, and tinkling away accompanying myself on the piano. So Joe Public got his money's worth from my 'turn' that Halloween and no mistake!

When I went gezzen I would dress up in any old clothes, like my father's boilersuit that he'd worn to the Yaird until it was worn out. My mother would cut the legs and arms down to size and just stick it all together with a belt. Or I'd get to borrow one of her cross-over aprons and tie a turban on my head. A mini Hilda Ogden if you will!

I did have a Chinese hat that had two long black pigtails attached to it that I wore for 'goin gezzen'. If I was wearing that hat my mother would get two long pieces of black wool, twirl them into two long droopy bits, then stick them to my face with sugar and water and make a long Mandarin-style moustache.

Or she'd scrape soot from the chimney and trail it over my face and hands, then get lipstick and smear it all over me as blood. I'd get to paint my nails with somebody's red nail varnish (which promptly came off before I went to school, much to my disgust). Then duly suited and booted as Dracula, off I'd go with my pals.

We'd knock on the neighbours' doors:

'Needin any gezzers?'
'Kin yeh dae a turn?'
'Yup!'
'Well, on yeh go. Let's hear it then.'

So you'd dance, sing, tell a joke, any old thing you thought was entertainment, and then you got a copper or two. But if it was some 'auld buddie' you usually just landed up with a sweetie, pancake or something like that.

After you'd gone round all the doors, it was home to count the spoils!

Up the West End there used to be a street called Bernard Street and I remember there being a huge street party there for a number of years, to celebrate the King's Coronation.

They would string bunting across the street between the tenements. Two kids were selected as the 'King and Queen', and there was a parade and they got 'crowned'. There would be tables laid out in the street with food and drink, and folk had a street party after the 'Coronation'.

This yearly event became quite famous and known throughout Dundee. I loved the Bernard Street parties I went to, and thought they were great fun! But in *my* house it was viewed in different ways.

My mother and us kids loved the whole thing and the excitement of it all, and looked forward to the Bernard Street 'Coronation Day' every year, when we could join in all the fun!

But my older brother would say he'd would rather die than be picked for the 'King' and have to, 'get a' ponced up like that.' This from the lad who was convinced a kilt was a skirt and no amount of 'Big strappin' Kilties who wore their kilts an looked smashin', or threats of 'Yeh'll dae whit yehr telt an' like it', ever persuaded him otherwise.

That's another famous adult-to-child contradiction; 'Dae whit yehr telt an like it!'

However, I do remember my mother giving in when my brother said he'd rather miss a wedding we'd been invited to, if he had to wear the kilt she'd bought him. So she must have known how miserable he felt about the whole kilt thing and getting 'ponced up' in general!

I leave the last word on our local 'Coronation Day' to my father, who never attended it anyway. His take on it was:

They [the Government] wid be better spendin' thir time and *oor* money trehin tae improve abodie's lot! Wir no needin any mair Keengs or Queens. But new hooses fir abody, a fraction o' the sehze o' 'that lot's' palace, might be a guid idea!

* * *

I'd like to finish up this chapter about fun and games by letting you in on a special wee memory about a magic trick that my father performed for me when I was a kid.

It took me to be able to tell the round side of a table knife from the flat side, before I solved this puzzle.

My father would cut six identical wee bits of paper from the border of the newspaper (no writing on it), then he'd stick three pieces of paper to the round side a table knife and three pieces to the flat side. Then he'd say:

'Dae yeh want tae see some real magic? Then watch me bla on these three buhts o' paper, an bla them right through the blade o' this steel knife!'

I did, of course, want to see this amazing feat, and for as many times as he would show me it.

He'd make a great pretence of huffing and puffing, all the while keeping the side of the knife that I could see, facing me. Then he'd whirl the knife about and twist it round right in front of my eyes, so that I could see he wasn't cheating.

Then with a mighty flourish he'd say:

'There yeh go, right through the knife! Jist like Eh telt yeh! Now that's real magic! An wiz that no clever?'

Very clever indeed in my opinion!

3

THE SKALE, 1940S STYLE

The first school I ever attended was Hawkhill Primary up the West End. From the day I walked through the door of that building I discovered one thing that was to remain with me for a long time: I loved the school!

I passed by a school the other day and all the kids were tearing around like wild Indians, and I had this sudden flashback to when we were kids and did exactly the same thing.

Nowadays, children are more officially protected which I think is a very good thing, but it did get me thinking about the differences (official and unofficial) when I was at primary school.

If someone picked on me back then, the cardinal rule from she-who-must-be-obeyed was I was to whack them right back! I was always told:

'Now mind! Dinna you ever hit furst, but if yeh get thumped, then gie them Tillinky'!

To this day I haven't a clue who or what 'Tillinky' was, but I sure knew what it meant as an action!

And on enquiring on what I would do if the kid was bigger than me I was informed:

'It's no the sehze o' yehr boadie! It's the sehze o' yehr heart! Stull gie them Tillinky!'

So 'Tillinky' it was! Disputes were settled there and then!

However, bullying was about the worst thing to be accused of in my neck of the woods, as I think it is to this day. And many a '*Look at the sehze o' him, hittin a wee thing like that*' took place between mothers in my street.

I was more fortunate than lots of my pals in having an older brother who thought he was John Wayne, so I had my own personal one-man posse to deal with any outlaws who waylaid me!

But, thankfully life in school was mainly about learning 'stuff' and having fun. And, of course, even way back then, hitting one another when we were in school was a big no-no!

When I first started school, our version of an electronic writing pad was a tin tray with sand in it. The teacher would write your ABCs on the board and you traced them in the sand, then shook the sand and practised all over again.

We had small abacuses to do our sums with and the units were identified by the bead colour.

I've always been a rotten speller and even worse at maths. I think that's why I warmed instantly to computers, who will spellcheck and do mathematics without even getting confused or fed up. But they can get you into their own kind of trouble.

I remember once writing a wee story for a retired union members' newsletter, and it must have said something about tatties and mince being a staple diet when we were kids. For the next week, when I was in town, one of the union members called me over as I passed by with a:

'Hey Mae! You must've been really poor whaur you lived lang ago!'

'Whit dae yeh mean?' I asked

'Well no mony o' us hid tae eat tatties an *"mice!"'*

And sure enough when I came home and looked at the article that's exactly what I'd written . . . and checked twice.

It's about on a par with the one where I was writing a wee bit about the 'sacred' cows in India and wrote *'scared'* instead. When that one was pointed out to me I had this vision of all the cows in India running up the closes shouting:

'Help iz! Help iz! Eh'm dead feart! The wind's near blahin iz awa!'

Anyway back to 1945-ish and school time!

I adored playing 'Hucky Duck' which meant any number of kids bending down and touching their toes, and the kids at the back leap-frogging over their shoulders, then that kid bent down at the front of the line and off they all went again.

I remember seeing one lad getting carted off to the school sickroom or wherever because his Hucky Duck line just kept moving forward and he leapt over the last in the lines' shoulders and headered smack dab right into the school wall.

'Meh Goad!' said my mother when I related this latest excitement after I got home that day. 'That laddie must need glesses right enough! Ee'll hae a heid the sehze o' a fufty shullin kale pot the moarn!'

I'm guessing here that a 'fufty shullin kale pot' referred to the same kind of pot as the huge black witches cauldron that bubbled eternally on our stove producing endless 'a-thin-in-it' soup. That pot provided my meal everyday as I dashed in the door at lunchtime. That and about a half loaf of bread!

To this day, I love homemade soup that you can stand a spoon up in. Nothing to beat it for 'stickin yehr ribs thegither' on a cold wintry day!

We played games called Tig (last man out), hide and seek, (still on the go), one potato, two potato, three potato, four and kissie catchie (an advanced game which included the boys and was only played once we got past the 'Yuk! Yeh've got tae be jokin. Nae weh am eh dain that!' stage).

When we got tired we would have a 'sittie on the dyke' (school wall), which was the kids' equivalent of a 'hingie oot the windie' or 'sittin haein a blether.'

And, of course, there was always your 'piecie' for playtime at school. We didn't have tuck shops back then, but my mother used to make puff candy, coconut squares, toffee (or a toffee apple) and we got a goodie for school everyday.

Back in my time, it was very much separate girls and boys games. There were a few 'lassies gemes' that were also domestic training and educational. My older sister remembers more about crocheting beddies than I do, and she was a dab hand at them.

'Beddies' were small squares, knitted with a crochet hook, from all the odd bits of wool that were left over. These squares were then sewn together to make bedcovers, pram covers, Tansad covers and shawls for the baby in its pram, or your granny when she was sitting in her chair at the fire in the winter.

My sister recalls that the girls (remember that playgrounds were segregated in those days) used to all sit along the wall at the school, all furiously crocheting away making their beddies. It was apparently great competition to measure how much you could do in one playtime and see who could make the biggest squares. So it was play with a purpose, for then all the squares were put to very good use and all the old odd bits of wool were recycled. I believe it's called 'structured' play nowadays!

These games were mainly for days when it rained. Then kids would all sit on the ground with their backs to the wall in the part of the playground that had a tin roof that kept the rain off.

I was never much of a knitter as a kid. I think it was because mainly, only your arms moved when you were knitting! But I do remember that I used to crochet slippers out of jute yarn that my granny brought home, and these were called 'Rovies'. I have no idea why they were named this, but I'm sure someone out there will have the answer.

Rovies would be called slipper socks nowadays, but jute was no soft cuddly material, and these Rovies were only for those who had really strong soles, or couldn't afford real 'Hoosies' (slippers). But my mother assured me that back when she was a kid, Rovies were very much a norm.

Anyway, I used to crochet away at these slippers, and then just unwind the jute and start again, while I had my real cosy slippers to keep me comfortable.

I do remember though that my pals and I crocheted 'Cattie-Tailies' as well.

For Cattie-Tailies you needed more old wool, a 'purn' (thread bobbin), a crochet hook and four wee nails. My mother would hammer the nails into the top of the purn (they were made out of wood back then). Then you cast four loops over the nails, pulled them through to the other end of the purn, and started making a great long skinny woollen tail, which could go from five inches to fifty inches depending on your wool or, in my case, your patience.

I think I made enough 'dish cloots' (dishtowels) to keep the Black Watch going in my time. Or I would wind the wool into a circle and it would be a teapot stand. Or I just made it bright and fancy, to tie up my hair.

Oh! And I remember cattie-tailing my long Mandarin whiskers for a dressie-up party I was going to!

So no wasted wool back in those days. And remember that knitting was as much a part of life back in the 1940s to 1950s as the Public Washing Houses (Washies), and loads of women 'hid somethin on the peens' (knitting needles) all the time.

Most of my school stuff was knitted. My great-auntie Mary was our chief 'wool person' and always had something on the go that she was knitting for us. She used to fair clickety-click with these knitting needles, like a human loom she was! She was also my older sister's main supplier of beddie wool.

Oh, and that was another use for the odds and ends of wool; darning socks and jumpers. My auntie Mary was a stickler for the darning wool being an exact match for the socks or jumpers she was darning. But I have seen some sights, when I was wee, I can tell you, if the kids' mother had to use any old odd spare wool for the darning. Some wee laddies even got their trousers darned with a different colour of wool.

When I asked my mother why this was she warned me:

Eh hope Eh niver catch you makin a fale o' ither bairns because o' whit thir wearin. If yehr covered an warm, then that's the main thing! An it's a whole lot better than goin aboot weh yehr elbows hingin oot o yehr jumper; yehr heels hingin oot o' yehr socks, or yehr e*** hingin oot o' yehr toarn breeks.

Fair do's! She got no argument from me, especially that bit about the toarn breeks!

Oh! And speaking of the word 'breeks'. Maybe I should explain here that 'breeks' to me can be either trousers or knickers!

I used to have thick, woollie type material, navy blue school knickers that had pockets in them. And I loved mine to bits. I could carry my hankie (no tissues back then) and my secret sweetie stash. In fact, I even carried a tiny matchbox-sized dollie in mine.

The bulge in my gymmie must have made me look like I had one leg that was twice as fat as the other.

My navy blue knickers doubled as gym shorts. No trainers or gym wear in those days, just your navy blue knickers 'an yehr 'sannies' (gym shoes) with the elastic in the sides of them!

Gym was accompanied, of course, on the school piano which always sounded out of tune to me, but I just skipped (or meleed) along to the music with the rest of the school knickers brigade (girls only, of course)!

A routine part of gym for me was when the teacher would shout across the hall:

Mary Stewart (my Sunday or 'dae-whit-yehr telt' name) get back in line!' Or 'Mary! Get back and hold your partner's hand! At once!

I still don't see the point of running around in an orderly queue, or being made to hold hands with someone who wasn't one of my pals, when I could be off doing my own thing!

Since schoolwear was always a blouse and a skirt or gymmie (gymslip if you went to the Academy along the road), or a dress of some type, you'd only to whip off your skirt/gymmie or dress, and there you were ready for the off.

If you were wearing a dress then you just had to stuff it into your knickers and leap about like you had battle-ship hips. When I think on this, we must have even worn our navy blue knickers under a frock! Help meh boab; these knickers must've been made out of magic material!

But (here's a great navy blue school knickers bonus) because these knickers were so big and roomy, it was absolutely:

'Nae bahther at a' tae pee through the leg o' yehr breeks!'

This was especially useful in winter time (for obvious reasons), or during playtime at school when wheeching your knickers up and down wasted good fun and games time!

Happy days right enough!

4

CHRISTMAS TREE! OH! CHRISTMAS TREE!

It was 1950. I'd been living in Fintry Housing Scheme in Dundee, with my family, for about a year, and our first Christmas in the 'new hoose' was approaching.

My mother decided she would push the boat out and we were all to set off for the Arcade in town to get a *really* good Christmas tree, now we had the room; 'we' being my wee brother (seven years), my wee sister (in the Tansad) and me (ten years). And leading the group, of course, the lady of the house.

We duly got off the bus at Shore Terrace and crossed the road to look at the trees that sat outside the door of the Arcade.

Well, there were big trees, wee trees, skinny trees and fat trees. Then she spots it and nudges me.

'Will yeh tak a look at that tree, now that's a real dinger!'

The 'real dinger' was just that. It was really, really green. It had a huge trunk. It was enormous. We fell in love with it.

'How much tae tak it aff yehr hands?' says she to the Arcade man, preparing for battle.

'Och! Well' says he. 'It's the same price as a' the rest, but yeh'll hae tae move it *now*, fir Eh canna store it fir yeh'.

'Done!' says my mother, as we nabbed the bargain of the year.

She turns to my brother and me.

'Tak meh bag, an ane o yeh haud the Tansad, till Eh get this tree manoeuvred across it.'

And in a couple of minutes my wee sister vanished under a pine forest, with just room for her to peek out on the world.

My mother issued directions.

'Ane o' yeh get the tap, an ane o' yeh get the bottom, tae balance it, till weh get tae the bus stop. Are yeh haudin on? Right aff weh go! Wagons Ho!'

We arrived at the bus stop and encountered our first hurdle. The bus conductor.

'Geezo Mrs, thir's nae weh that things comin' on the bus.'

'Says wha?'

'The sehze o' the bus says; that's wha! Fir Eh'll no get it in the cubbie.'

And he was right. Try as he might, it would not go in 'the Cubbie'.

'Right!' says my mother to us. 'Then weh'll jist hae tae get the tram car an' walk fae Maryfield.'

By this time it was getting dark, and I was beginning to go off this tree big time and we were all getting weary, but the 'get-the-tree-hame' mission had to be accomplished. We were after all speaking about my mother. Anyway, we got this giant of a thing on the tramcar right enough. The tram conductor had to fold down two rows of seats, muttering away to anybody who'd listen; 'Guid joab it's no' the busy time.' He just got ignored.

Fifteen minutes later, when we got to the terminus at the top of the Forfar Road, it had started to pour down that damp feechy sleet.

'Nearly hame now,' says mother, convincing none of the troops.

My wee brother walked on uncomplaining but getting very downcast. I got thumped for mumping about my gloves getting soaked and me having cold fingers, and was instructed to: 'Bla on them, we'll be hame afor yeh kin say Jeck Roabson.' I was too tired to care about any Jeck Roabson, whoever he was, as we trudged on.

The only happy one was my sister. She was wrapped up like a wee bird, nesting in the tree. And she did look like a bird with all the pine cones sticking to her pink, fluffy angora bonnet and matching mitts.

Finally, we arrived home!

My father must've been looking out for us because he was at the door when we got there.

'Whit the hells that? Sherwood Forest?

'Whit the hell diz it look like? An niver mind a' that, jist help iz get it in the hoose.'

'An Mary, how dae yeh suggest Eh get a *twelve tae fourteen fuht* tree intae a hoose that's only *ten fuht* fae the flair tae the ceilin?'

She stopped dead. I stopped dead. My wee brother burst into tears. My sister, the wee pink bird, was oblivious . . . lucky her.

We'd humphed that tree for what seemed the same distance as it took Hannibal to get his elephants over the Alps. AND IT WAS TOO BIG!

So we small group of pioneers stood looking out the living room window as my father sawed off the extra feet and re-pinned the bottom of the tree to its crossed wooden slats, then dragged it through the door and stood it up in the living room.

'Och now, admit it, diz that no look jist smashin?' enthused my mother, beaming at all and sundry, including the tree.

'Nae herm done. It widda been worse if it hid been too wee.'

5

THE ARCADE

When you walk through the open tunnel that leads off to the right, at the bottom of the escalator from Tayside House, you pass by a few offices and a car park. When I was young the area round the 'Arcade' was a bustling hive of activity and was alive with Dundonians during the weekend.

I have this feeling that the Arcade never opened seven days a week, and that the shops inside shut on some weekdays, but six days a week you could use the Arcade as a short cut from the town to the main bus stance.

You could enter the Arcade from two directions. One was down the steps that leads off the City Square and into another tunnel that leads on to Castle Street. At the bottom of the stairs, there is a door on the right (now old and desolate). Behind that door there are three or four flights of stairs that led into the Arcade.

Speaking about Castle Street, I wonder if there are some of you who do not know that there used to be a theatre there, and that if you stand across the road where the grocer shop is now, and look high up at the building across the street, you'll see a bust of William Shakespeare sitting in a carved-out circular space in the wall. Yes you will and right in the middle of Dundee! So if you haven't already discovered this, then go and have a wee nosey for yourself!

If I read in the newspapers, after this book comes out, that some folk were bumping into each other in Castle Street, because it would appear they all staring upwards at the walls, then I'll know it's my fault!

Anyway that's just an aside. Back to the Arcade.

Arcade entry number two came off the road outside that's parallel with Shore Terrace. Back then the other side of the pavement, which is now a car park and Tayside House, was the local bus station and all the buses that went back and forth to the schemes, and other parts of Dundee, left from there. So the through road that the Arcade provided, gave access to and from the town and the bus station.

Inside the Arcade was an amusement centre that had penny slot machines and a machine with a metal hook for picking up some wee present. Oh, and a machine that you put a penny in it and a ghost popped out of a coffin to scare you. That paltry wee ghost would have lasted two minutes in the Princess Cinema up the West End where I used to live. The beast with five fingers would've had him back in his coffin in no time!

There was a palmist machine that you held your hand over the pad, and then a lot of tiny needles (with rubber ends I may add) rolled up and down your hand. The machine then dropped a card into a slot attached to its side, and you had a reading of your past, present and future, which, of course, promised you love with the man of your dreams (even when you were nine or ten), long life and plenty of everything, including money.

Sometimes your card told you to beware of a dark-haired stranger who would cross your path, or to look out for danger in the month of June. I suppose that meant that if a tall, dark stranger broke your leg in June, then you'd got your money's worth!

I used to love getting my palm read by that machine, and on enquiring of 'She-who-knows-everything-in-the-world' if it was true that the lines in your hand were your fortune, because that was what the machine said, my mother replied:

'Well that's a load o' rubbish tae spend yehr coppers on! Meanwhile afore weh a get rich quick, geez a hand weh they bags tae the bus.'

I still got my palm read when I had the money!

Some Saturdays we would use our pennies to go and play the slot machines. Then we would be cautioned with:

'Well when it's gone, it's gone! An dinna come back fir any mair. The only ane gettin rich here is that mannie ower there.'

'That Mannie' had the big leather bag that gave out change if it was required. He never looked rich to me I have to say!

There was also a kids play area in the Arcade. I remember there was this see-saw that had the ugliest child-sized elf (who was made out of plaster of Paris) balanced on one end of the see-saw. He had a red hat, and ears twice the size of his head and the hat put together!

You put your kid on the other end of the see-saw from Eddie (our name for him), then put money in the slot and off you went into the wild blue yonder with Eddie the Elf and his big fixed 'stookie' (plaster of Paris) smile!

I bet Eddie wished he could've had *his* palm read, and then he'd have seen into the future, where he had two chipped ears, half a nose, both his eyes peeling, a chipped and faded red hat and scabby green trousers. And on seeing all that Eddie could've jumped off the Arcade see-saw beforehand and run away with a circus before he was knocked to bits by a thousand small Dundonians!

I think Eddie was also there to earn his keep by allowing only one kid at a time on his see-saw. But I have often been passing by and seen some poor wee kid shoved in front of Eddie, with the bigger kid on the other end, so that they both 'got a hurl fir the same thruppence!'

I don't remember there being a 'ane-at-a-time' guy looking after Eddie, so he just had to put up with some kid being jammed in front of him. However, there was always a queue for Eddie, so it just goes to show that kids don't give a monkey about appearances if they like you!

* * *

That reminds me. My youngest sister had a doll somebody had knitted for her, and it would've scared the daylights out of a six-foot Viking, but she loved it to bits! It had great big popping, stitched eyes and a huge red mouth, like the Bride of Chuckie. My mother tried losing it; all hell broke loose. She tried hiding it before we went out; all hell broke loose. She tried saying things to my sister like, 'bad dahllie! Bad Dahllie!' before she handed it to her in her Tansad in the hope of putting her off; all hell broke loose and real tears flowed. So in the end, Bride of Chuckie went everywhere until she was reduced to a faded washed and chewed-up ball of jumbled wool, and my wee sister outgrew her, and she really was 'Chuckie' then! Right in the bin!

* * *

There was a tea shop in the Arcade where you could get snacks like stovies, soup in a cup, scones, toast and a drink. I think it used to have these red and white checked plastic tablecloths. My mother used to love the scones they made there!

If memory serves me there was also a fortune-telling booth that was kept quite busy at the weekend, but that was adults only. I can't remember the fortune teller's name but it would be Madam 'Eh-ken-athin' or something like that.

My mother's take on fortune tellers (in the Arcade or anywhere else) was:

It's worse than that palm machine! Thir only gein a shullin awa! If anybody could tell yeh yehr future, then how are they no sittin' in great big hooses an livin the life o' Reilly, instead o' sittin' in a wee booth in the Arcade in Dundee? Anywey wha the hell wahnt's tae be bahthered weh the future? Eh've enough tae dae weh the here an now!

So although folk went in and out of the fortune teller's booth, and there was sometimes even a queue, she never got 'meh mither's shullin.'

As for Reilly, I guess he lived in the same street as Jeck Roabson, the man who was the fastest guy in town according to my mother, no matter what you did. Example:

'Never mind moanin aboot the cleanin', get on weh it an yeh'll be feenished afore yeh kin say Jeck Roabson!'

Or:

'Weh'll get back intae the toon fir the pehs an bridies an hame agen afore yeh kin say Jeck Roabson!'

To this day I do not know who Reilly or Jeck Roabson were, but they were quoted regularly as examples in my life!

There were various other shops in the Arcade: a fruit shop; a china and ornaments shop; a sweetie shop, a shop that sold chickens that were roasted on a spit, and you could buy a half-chicken as well (many a Saturday night tea that provided for Dundonians!). There was a butcher's and a shop that sold linoleum. In fact the Arcade was a real wee hive of industry.

Outside the Arcade at the Shore Terrace end there was a photographer who had a monkey and would take your picture with the monkey. I have to say that as a kid I never liked monkeys that weren't behind bars! They shrieked too loudly and dived too fast for me, and the first monkey I met was up at my grandfather's hen run at the bottom of the Law Hill, and he hated me, but not half as much as I hated him back!

Anyway lots of kids and adults got their photo taken with this monkey. And I'll bet some Dundonians have monkey photos lying in a box to this day!

At the weekends, the Arcade would catch all the passing trade that went from the town to the bus stance at Shore Terrace.

Also outside the Shore Terrace end of the Arcade was a man who used to play the melodeon. His melodeon had a wire with a wee canvas bag attached to the end of it, and he was there every weekend, in rain, hail or snow. What sticks in my mind about this man was that no matter the weather he never had any socks on, and his shoes were always pot black with dirt.

My mother always used to give him some money and she was known at times, to stick one of our pies (still hot) into his hand as well. When I enquired why he never had any socks (funny what's important to a kid) my mother would just say:

'Because eez no as lucky as us. An that's how weh gie him a wee help when weh kin.'

At least the Accordion Man played a whole lot better than the Penny Whistle Man who played just outside Markies, who in my opinion couldn't play that whistle to save himself. But on the other hand he did dance as well!

There were loads of buses outside the Arcade, for bear in mind that you could've been loaded down until your arms were near trailing the ground and it wouldn't have entered your mind to get a taxi! And very few people I knew back then owned a car, so buses ran to all parts of Dundee, at regular intervals.

Also the bus on Saturday was sometimes like a mobile 'Washie' with all the women who lived in Fintry getting on the bus with their shopping and their kids as extra bearers.

One of my jobs when I was old enough was to go with my mother and help 'tae kerry the messages'. My pennies for the slots in the Arcade and the goodies from the sweetie shop weren't handed out for nothing!

* * *

Nowadays, I get off the bus regularly at Tayside House, to go to the Olympia Centre for some exercise and a swim each week. Some of the buildings in Shore Terrace are closed. Some of them are in use as offices. The back door to the Caird Hall is of course still very much in use for entertainment venues. Folk use the tunnel as they come in and out of Tayside House, and cut along to Castle Street or the town.

As I go along Shore Terrace, instead of saying hello to the Arcade photographer and his wee monkey dressed up like Sinbad the Sailor, or the Melodeon Mannie, I say a quick hello to the Big Issue seller who stands at the bottom of the escalator!

One day, as I came down the Tayside House escalator and

turned right, there was a wind blowing through the tunnel. That's not an unusual occurrence, but this day the tunnel, for no reason whatsoever, felt like one of those whispering galleries.

So I stopped to listen, and 'feel' what used to be here, on this street, before the tunnel and Tayside House were even there.

As I stood looking at the old buildings that used to be so alive, I felt a bit sad. There was an old newspaper stuck in one of the doorways and everything looked a dull grey. In my mind's eye, I pictured all the shops, and all the bustle of the weekends that took place on this very spot. I glanced along at the door that was once the entrance to the Arcade and thought back to what a busy thoroughfare it was when I was young.

I visualised my mother and my brother or sister as we made our way home at the weekend through the Arcade, or down Crichton Street or Castle Street, and along Shore Terrace for our bus, after getting the Saturday pies, bridies and chocolate Duchess Cake from Wallace's Pie Shop for the Saturday lunch.

I pictured us when we went into the Arcade for something to eat, to keep us 'going' until we got home, after we'd come out the old Victorian swimming baths that stood where the Olympia stands now, having been 'fir-a-dook' with my father.

I remembered all the folk passing through that one wee area outside the Arcade and the stance across the road that housed most of Dundee's buses.

I pictured once again the Arcade at Christmas time, with the trees leaning against the wall outside, where we picked our first big 'real' Christmas tree for Fintry.

So, I just said a quick hello and cheerio to all the ghosts

hovering around in the tunnel and went on my way across the car park to the one multi-service bus stop still 'alive' on Shore terrace.

As I stood at the bus stop the cars, buses and lorries were all whizzing over the road bridge where once the Empress Ballroom and the impressive entry to the King George VI (I think it was) Wharf used to be.

I glanced back and the Arcade was back to being just . . . Shore Terrace.

Then my bus came round the corner, so I stuck out my hand, got on the bus with my concession ticket (something they wouldn't have dreamed of back in the 1940s or 1950s), pulled myself back into the twenty-first century and made my way home.

6

WE KENT HOW TAE BEHAVE WHEN EH WIZ YOUNG

Did you hear yourself in that chapter heading? Then I guess you're in my age group or near enough! But, after a conversation I had with my sister, I have come to the conclusion that all behaviour is relevant!

I remarked on the fact that my pals and I had little money, but we had a great time when we were teenagers. As long as we had enough for the ice rink and the dancing, we were hunky-dorey! When I look back we were always laughing. And we just minded our own business, and we never did anybody any harm!

My sister looked at me:

Well! Eh kin only speak aboot you! Yeh're right that yeh wir niver in any real trouble. Yeh're also dead right that maist o' the time yeh were always jumpin aboot laughin. But yeh wir an absolute nightmare at times. Mum had to cover up fir yeh half the time, an the other half, Dad jist aboot had a fit cause yeh wid not dae whit yeh wir telt! But that only seemed to stop you for about two minutes. Talk aboot Scarlet O'Hara!

I had to laugh! 'Tae see oorsels as ithers see us' right enough! I never thought I caused too much trouble as a kid. You see When I was between five and fifteen years of age, my mother and particularly my father, knew everything. And my father could solve any problem, no matter what. And his word was law as far as I was concerned!

But by the time I'd reached fifteen years of age, I was amazed that I could have ever thought that they knew everything, and decided that that should be my role from then on. From the age of twenty, the roles changed completely. I was making my own decisions (and mistakes) but I could always count on their council, and their unswerving support to help me in any way they could.

When my father died (I was aged thirty-five) and my mother was now on her own, our relationship changed yet again.

* * *

By the time I was forty-five life had taken us both full circle and I was now the one helping my mother with her decision-making!

However, as I grow older, a really strange thing has happened! The older I get, the more my parents seem to know! I sometimes think I'm morphing into my father, the things I come away with these days.

So here's the conclusion I've come to. No matter how things change, some things always remain the same!

Anyway as for the 'yeh-wir-jist-a-nightmare' conversation I had with my sister, it made me think about some of these 'nightmares'.

* * *

In the mid-fifties, one of my best pals lived in the next street from mine in Fintry, and she had an older sister as well. My other best pal lived up the Hilltown, and she had brothers but no sisters! She was always (well not always, but nearly always) the voice of reason that just got ignored, but she stuck up valiantly for us just the same! Still does!

My pal who lived up 'The Hulltoon', (not to be mixed up with the 'Hullie' which was a cemetery) used to listen to my other pal and me going on about how unreasonable our big sisters could be, especially when it came to sharing 'our' things, (which meant us 'borrowing' their stuff). And although she never had that as a problem, she understood and sympathised with us completely!

My father hated debt of any kind (if he hadn't been bald, he'd have had a curly perm without paying for it nowadays) and that was why the 'new blue coat incident' which took place was a big deal!

In our house, no one was allowed to 'tak a turn oot o' a Clubbie book' (catalogue), never mind McGills Lines (credit), or a Provie' (Provident Insurance Company) cheque. Owing any of the grocery shops money was also not on. In my father's world, 'Yeh beh whit yeh kin afford, or yeh wait until yeh kin afford it.'

Alright for him! He'd never seen the most absolutely beautiful, had-to-have coat in this neighbour's catalogue that I'd spotted one day when she was in visiting my mother. It was the bees knees, this coat; nipped in at the waist and had about a hundred yards of material flowing out from there. It would cover skirts and dresses perfectly that 'were in' at that moment. It just had one minor draw back! I'd no money!

I set about working on my mother;

'Ma how kin Eh no get a turn oot o' this Clubbie book? Eh could afford tae pey it up every week.'

'Yeh! Right! You that's niver got twa huppenies tae rub thegither! An yeh ken the answer tae that afore yeh ask it.'

So that seemed to be the end of that, until Mrs Clubbie-book left!

'Kin weh no dae it an jist no tell meh Dad?'

'Eh dinna ken if that's a guid idea.'

After much wheedling and debate (and doubts on my mother's part) it was decided that my mother would sign for this coat that cost about £6. I would go each Friday after my work to this woman's house and give Mrs Clubbie-book half a crown until it was paid up. We would tell my father, if he even noticed the coat, that I'd had it for ages. And no one (my father in other words) need be any the wiser!

I have to stop here and tell you about something my father once said to me many years later:

Yehr Mither an you must've thought Eh wiz deaf, dumb, blind an then half daft. Yeh'd gae intae the toon! Yeh'd come back weh bags. She'd come intae the livin room twitterin awa like a budgie. You'd belt up the stairs, an come back doon bagless. Then later on you'd appear weh somethin new on. An a' this performance wiz aboot me no tellin yeh tae get lost when yeh'd nae money later on in the week, an got maist o' yehr board money back aff yehr Mither.

Anyway, the fancy new blue coat . . .

It was the biz and much admired by all my pals. It was just like Audrey Hepburn's in her latest film! The difference being Audrey Hepburn could have afforded it!

Then one fine day, I forgot to go to Mrs Clubbie-book's house to pay my weekly debt and just pranced off gaily, to wherever, to enjoy myself.

The woman's husband, who knew nothing of the 'pey-the-coat-up-an'-no-let-on-tae-father' subterfuge, and who was the one who went round the doors on Friday night for his wife, collecting the money owed on the books, noticed I'd not paid, and arrived innocently at our front door.

Now ... who do you think answered the door? Yup! You've got it in one! I'll have to give you my mother's take on his bit of the story as I was out on my merry travels with not a care in the world.

So my father opens the door,

'Oh! Hello there. Whit kin Eh dae fir yeh?'

'Hello! Eh've come fir the half croon yehr lassie owes fir ehr clubbie this week.'

'Eh'm sorry but yehr at the wrang hoose. Thir's nae "tick" in this hoose!'

My mother had appeared at the back of him the moment she heard the word 'tick' (money owed), and was, by this time, I would imagine trying to work out how she could stop the proverbial 'you-know-what' hitting the fan!

'Oh! Hello there. Eh'm jist elling yehr man Eh'm up fir meh wife's Clubbie money. Yehr lassie must've forgotten tae come tae the hoose weh it!'

My father looked at my mother. My mother said not a word. The man looked at the both of them. My father broke the silence.

'How much is owed? An what's it owed on?'

'Well now; wait tull Eh look at the book? Eh! It's a coat! An thir's three pounds an fehve shullins left tae clear it aff, but twa an six the night.'

'Hud on! Mary gie this man eez wife's money oot the "tin".'

The 'tin' was our emergency money. In those days we also had a saving book as well, (riches indeed) but the 'tin' held money for something that 'cropped up an yeh didna expect it!' Well that man coming to our door that night certainly fitted the bill.

My mother gave him the outstanding money. My father demanded a receipt, then informed this poor man, who I guess by now just wanted to get away as fast as possible.

'Sorry aboot this, but that's the debt cleared! An now! Let me tell yeh something. Eh don't want tae see you, or yehr wife, or any bliddy Clubbie books near this door agen! Hiv yeh got that?'

With that, Mrs Clubbie-book's husband got dismissed, to go home and tell his wife what had happened. I would imagine Mrs Clubbie-book dodged my mother for a few weeks, even though it wasn't her fault.

And my father sat at the fire 'nursing his wrath tae keep it warm' while he decided how he'd deal with me. My mother, protector of us all, was also not daft and abandoned me to my fate.

I came traipsing home from wherever, the owed money still not even in my thoughts. I'd forgotten it altogether, so I opened the front door and walked right into ... my new, pale blue, fitted fancy coat lying on the hall floor like a carpet! Ting! Then I remembered right enough that I'd forgotten to go to Mrs Clubbie-book's house and pay my debt ... followed hard on its heels by the reality that *she'd come to mine!*

Then I looked up and there was my father just standing at the living room door, with my mother at the back of him making silent slicing motions across her throat! As if I needed anybody to tell me to keep my mouth shut and not to ask what my coat was doing on the floor.

I will not fill three pages telling you the lecture I got on being selfish and taking money out of the emergency tin for what was *definitely* not an emergency, so I'd better hope that no one else in the house had a *real* emergency (No guilt there then). I was to start paying the money back into the tin at the same rate as I would have paid for the coat *all on my own* (he emphasised that bit). Worst of all, I had gone behind his back!

I resisted any temptation to utter a word! Life was as precious to me then as it is now! My mother poured oil on the troubled waters, and dealt with things in her own way as usual. But I definitely *did* have to pay back every penny of my fancy coat into the tin.

On that fateful night however, when the dust settled, and we were on our own, I remember her saying to me;

'Ach niver mind. Athin'll be fine! An yeh've stull got yehr coat. Weh kin aye get it cleaned.'

Even though I'd been the one to nag her into letting me get the coat and the ensuing embarrassment that followed, she was still on my side.

But you know what? I never did get much joy out of that coat from then on!

As for my father? Well he had his rules and he was right; I never should have done that with the coat business!

It took me a wee while to forgive myself for the upset I had caused, but I was young and life quickly carried me into another adventure.

My father died before the advent of real kiddy-on plastic money. I wonder what he'd think nowadays?

* * *

Oh! And there was the saga of my pal; who lived down the road, and her sister's new frock.

My pal's sister was a great dressmaker and used to make lots of her own clothes. One night, I called down at their house, I suppose to pick up my pal, and then jump on a bus to go meet the other part of the trio, and hop off to the dancing.

When I arrived and we both went upstairs so she could finish getting ready, we went into her room and she pointed at this dress lying on the bed. It was lovely.

It had a huge full skirt and a top that had a peplum at the waist, so that it looked like a blouse over a skirt. My pal says to me:

'She dizzna like it! She's feenished weh it!'

'She dizzna like it. Whit's wrang weh it?'

'The hem's a wavy.'

'Kin she no fix it?'

'No. Eh dinna think so!'

Then my pal had this great idea.

If the dress was now 'useless to her sister, then maybe *she* could make some use of it! Now this is where one of us should have gone and asked! But that would've been too simple!

So she decided to cut the skirt off the dress underneath the peplum bit and make it into a blouse! Clever idea I thought! So she did! And you know what? It worked a treat! This dress turned into an absolutely lovely blouse. I complimented her on being so clever, and asked if I could borrow the blouse for the dancing the next time.

So off we trotted out the door saying cheerio to her mum and here's the bit I find priceless when I look back. My pal never even hid the remains of the dress, and I never even thought that she should. She just flung it over the bottom of the bed. I suppose the logic of that was that her mother, who had an even better 'pair o' hands' than her sister, could make something out of the 'remnant'.

Had she but *asked* anybody, we would've discovered that

her sister was to be altering the dress so that the hem would *not* be wavy! Well, I can tell you the 'wavy' problem had been solved in earnest, with the snip of the scissors! Can you picture her sister's face when she went upstairs to get her new frock and found a topless skirt lying on the bed instead?

Suffice to say that justice was meted out and my pal had to pay her sister back all the money for the frock!

I used to borrow my sister's clothes without asking, when I could get away with it. And always got caught out!

All these acts brought retribution of some kind or another, but the memories only lasted until the next antic (Scarlet O'Hara right enough)!

The rule in my house was that if I wanted to borrow any of my sister's clothes, I had to ask her permission first. But if I'd asked, I would've got an almighty 'no!' So what was the point in asking?

We used to do things that would've had some of today's social workers say we were dysfunctional! Thank goodness we never knew what that was.

I should point out here, that we didn't have lots of clothes-changes back then, and there was no Primark in my days, where you could get loads of outfits for next to nothing.

* * *

By now my relationship with my older brother was completely changing and we were going our separate ways. Sure we still had laughs. Like the time he saw me coming along the road and as the house was empty and there was no one to watch this antic, he hauled himself up into the loft and hid there! Upstairs in our house we had a row of coat hooks along the wall that was just onder the loft door. So when I was hanging my coat up he just leapt down from the loft and nearly scared the living daylights out of me! Good job I didn't have a dicky heart, then he'd have been sorry!

Nowadays, in our new grown-up relationship, I would iron his shirts and polish his shoes for him, and he would always bung me 'dancing money' if I was skint, which was an everyday occurrence for me! But now the monkeyshines I had shared with him when we were kids were replaced with new monkeyshines; with my pals!

My pals were now my mentors and that suited me fine, for they usually agreed with me! And we all agreed about the injustices that were meted out to us when we were getting into trouble. After all, weren't we grown up now, and didn't need a lot of advice!

And that attitude led me quite nicely on to what I will call the 'clean up yehr bedroom' saga.

In my house we all had 'oor ain cleanin joabs'. These were tasks that helped my mother out. When you got old enough to dig in and help, you were required to do just that!

But as we all know some things are eternal and teenagers doing domestic tasks, or even cleaning up after themselves is, and always has been, a universal battle.

I shared a bedroom with my older sister until she left to get married. And since I saw our bedroom as 'oor domain', then keeping the place tidy and clean came second to diving out the door to enjoy myself!

We had a round basket chair in the corner of the bedroom that I used as a wardrobe! I also threw my shoes under the same chair. The dressing table looked like a war zone with all my make-up and other accoutrements! And I dodged taking my turn making the bed (sheets and blankets and top covers back then) as often as I could.

My sister would, of course, complain constantly to my

mother, (quite right), who would then get hold of me and say:

'Wull you clean up that pig steh o' a chair. Thir must be a died boady leyin in that coarner beh now?'

Or:

'Dae you think yehr sister's yehr skiffie? Well Eh'm tellin yeh . . . She's no! Get that room cleaned up!'

Or:

'Eh'm seek fed up speakin tae you aboot that room! Eh'm gonna land up tellin yehr father on yeh, an see whit happens then!'

Meanwhile, my sister got so cheesed off with the whole bedroom 'thing' that she decided to take action of her own. She came from my house remember!

She decided that she would clean one half of the room and just leave me to do whatever I wanted to in my half! And that's just what she did!

She dusted one half of the dressing table, and piled my stuff up on the other to 'jist gether stoor'. She made one half of the bed (Oh, yes you can, for she did it), and just left my half all crumpled up! She moved my wardrobe-chair over into what she had now christened 'my half of the room' and just bunged everything on top of it! Then she hovered and dusted her half bedroom!

Okey dokey! It suited me! I was far too busy with other much more important things and, as long as I had clean underwear and clothes, and could find my make-up and earrings etc., I was happy with the arrangement that had shut my sister up, and I could just clean my half of the room when I had the time.

WRONG!

After a week or two of this, my mother went absolutely nuts at the state my half of the room was in!

In my house my mother dealt with most 'non-high offences' concerning us, but that didn't mean my father had lost the use of his ears and was ignorant of what was going on.

So one day . . . I got the summons:

'Right! Eh'm no yehr mither! Eh'm no askin yeh! Eh'm tellin yeh! The day, *if not sooner*, you wull get up they stairs an clean up that room. Or face the consequences! Do Eh mak mesel clear?'

I had known my father all my life, but if I remember I was going somewhere very important like the ice rink or the dancing that night, and since it would take the whole day and into half the night to really clear up the place to the satisfaction of 'he-wha-really-means-it' I begged my mother's help with this problem:

'Tell Dad Eh promise Eh'll get really stuck in the moarn, an the room'll be shinin like a bubble when Eh'm feenished!'

'Like that's gonna happen? Well Eh've an even better idea. You tell him *yehrsel!* Cause Eh'm the ane that feenished! Feenished weh a' this kerryin ons! Dae yeh ken what; sometimes you're jist like bliddy Walter Mitty! So . . . be it on yehr ain heid!'

Even my own mother had deserted me! Plan 'A' had not had its usual outcome!

So on to plan 'B'. I would just throw everything into the real wardrobe out of sight, and then I'd do my proper clean-up the very next day. So if my father went into the room when I was out he'd think I'd started, and that should be alright!

WRONG AGAIN!

But I did it anyway. I just skimmed over the dust on my half of the dressing table with my nightie and bunged everything in sight into the wardrobe. Then off I went. Job well done!

When I arrived back home it would have been around about ten o'clock at night. I just shouted my usual, 'It's me. Hi-Ya!' Then dived upstairs, to get out of my good clothes and into my old skivvies.

* * *

That 'It's me. Hi-Ya!' reminds me of when we all got to the age that we went out on our own and came back later on in the evening, and my parents and the two youngest members of my family had gone to bed. We'd come in and as we gently shut the door my mother would shout down the stairs:

'Wha's that?'

'It's me!' (Each of us replied, 'It's me').

'Okay then! Dinna mak a noise!'

And in my older brother's case.

'An dinna eat whit's in the pot (or casserole), that's the moarn's dehner. An dinna drink a' the milk!' (You will have gathered that my brother could have eaten us out of house and home).

She did this 'wha-is-it? Check' with each of us, as she couldn't get to sleep until we were all in. In later years, my father was to recall these check-ins by saying:

'Dinna mak a noise! Dinna eat the dehner! Dinna drink the milk! Eh'd her shoutin in meh ear until yeh wir a' back in the hoose, then she jist drapped aff tae sleep in twa meenits, efter makin mair noise than anybody.'

* * *

Anyway back to the upstairs landing after I'd arrived home having dodged away without cleaning up my half of the bedroom.

I entered the bedroom to find . . . ABSOLUTELY NOTHING!

It was like I didn't live in this room anymore! Even my wardrobe-chair was gone! I dived frantically over to the real wardrobe and opened the door. I'd gone from there too! Plan 'B' seemed to have failed miserably.

So I dived back downstairs into the living room, where my mother and father sat, reading their books or papers.

'Hi-Ya!' (my Mother)

'So yehr in?' (my Father)

'Meh stuff's a' gone!' (guess who?)

My father put his book down:

'Whit a' that rubbish that's been leyin aboot fir ages? That naebody seems tae want, or look efter. Och! Eh jist threw it oot!'

'Yeh threw it oot?'

'Yup! It's a' at the bin.'

'It's a' at the BIN!'

'Is thir somethin wrang weh your hearin?

Something told me the conversation was at an end! Here's what had happened while I was out.

My father had heard the door bang earlier as I had dived out the door with a quick 'cheerio' to my mother. So he'd gone upstairs to inspect the bedroom, returned and said to my mother:

'Is she awa oot fir the night?'

'Yup!'

'Right!'

Then without another word he departed into the kitchen, came back with some black bin liners, went into my bedroom and dumped everything he could lay hands on into the bags, put everything out onto the top landing, opened the landing window and turfed all my stuff out the window. He even cleared my side of the dressing table!

Then he came downstairs with my wardrobe-chair, went out the back door and threw my wardrobe-chair and the rest of the bags into the bin recess!

So now we return to his immortal words: 'Yup! It's a' at the bin.' And me standing there in a state of disbelief!

'Since yeh'd time tae gae oot, Eh jist assumed yeh wir feenished! So Eh went up tae see how the room had shaped up! When Eh saw it, Eh thought Eh'd gie yeh a hand weh movin a' the rubbish that wiz leyin aboot, so yeh could feenish aff the cleanin that yeh'd left.

'But if any o' that auld junk that wiz leyin on the chair or the flair o' the wardrobe, or litterin the tap o' the dressin table's any use tae yeh, an yeh want any o' it back afore the scaffies (cleansing officers if we'd lived in the Ferry) come, Eh'd dae it now if Eh wir you!

'But don't bring that chair back intae this hoose!'

So that's exactly what I did! And on my own!

I got a torch and collected all the bin bags, carried them back up the stairs and piled them up in the space in the corner of the room that used to have a very nice wardrobe-chair in it. And the next day, I got stuck into the cleaning in earnest, and got things back to 'normal'.

So it's my father's fault that from that day to this, I cannot leave things hanging over the back of a chair!

* * *

Oh! Then there was one Friday night when we were all trying to get ready to go out at once! My older brother had already aggravated my father by standing at the mirror in the living room and combing his DA, and keeping all the heat of the fire from the rest of the room!

Then I started to argue with my sister about who'd get the hair dryer first or something like that.

My brother had the record player in his room up too loud (for my father) as he was getting ready to go out.

Then suddenly the whole place went into complete silence and darkness!

Minutes passed and we were still in the dark (literally)!

So where was my father (the electrician) to sort this electrical fault?

I went into the living room and there he was, sitting with his wife and they were each reading their papers with a . . . TORCH!

There hadn't been a fuse. My father had switched the lights off at the mains. He rose from his chair with:

'Now! Eh'm gonna switch they lights on agen, an if you lot canna get ready like civilised human bein's, then Eh'm gonna switch them aff! An yeh kin a' get ready tae go oot in the bliddy dark!'

As I write this I have to smile. The fact that my mother just went and got a torch when he 'lost it,' and switched off the electricity at the mains, is something that was considered normal in our house!

But you know what? We all got ready without any uproar and they got peace to read their papers!

* * *

Nowadays, I like the place to be clean and tidy, although I wouldn't get house person of the year award.

One of my 'things' is that I like the cushions plumped and the pictures on the wall hanging straight! It drives me nuts if a picture's squint.

I recall one night, many years ago, when my father was up at my house and he was rawl-plugging the wall so that I could hang this new picture I had bought, and I said to him:

'Dad that wa's a wee bit on the squint so yeh might hae tae yaze yehr plumb tae mak share that the picture'll hing strecht?'

'Are yeh tellin me how tae rawl plug a wa' an hing a picture?'

'No! But yeh ken whit Eh'm like if it dizzna hing right!'

'Eh! An Eh also mind when the stoor could've been meetin yeh comin oot o' that bedroom door, an yeh'd jist hae jumped ower it, niver mind "Is meh picture gonna hing strecht?" Cheenged days eh?'

'Eh! An mind when you flung a' meh stuff oot the windie. When Eh think aboot it, you wir quite hard on me back then.'

'Hard on yeh? *Hard on yeh?* Yehr bliddy lucky yeh hid yehr mither tae cover up fir yeh half the time! Or else Eh might hae threw you oot the windie as well!'

Later on, after he'd finished the job, and we sat having a cup of tea and a pancake in jam (one of his favourites), he pointed at the picture;

'Is that strecht enough fir yeh?'

'Well . . .' says I, 'Wid Eh dare tae say it wizzna? Eh'm fower storeys up!'

7

THE WEEK WEH WENT TAE ROTHESAY-OH!

It was around about June or July in 1956 or 1957, and I was about to embark on another new adventure for me. I was going on holiday with my pals, all on my own, for the first time. Our destination was to be the far outer reaches of Rothesay, for one whole week!

Talk about excitement! I was as high as a kite about the whole thing!

Back in those days, Rothesay was the Riviera of the West Coast and was one of Scotland's most popular holiday destinations; a mini Benidorm if you will, but much colder and wetter, so you never had to worry about sunstroke or getting malaria or anything like that. You might get frostbite, but that was only if you'd travelled up from some far outer regions like the south of England.

If memory serves me, one of us looked up the holiday destinations in the papers and we phoned and booked ourselves into a boarding house that we could afford.

To save money we booked what was described as a family room at the top of the house, and we were assured it would certainly hold the number we required.

So we duly sent a postal order with the deposit and secured our first 'goin-on-yehr-own' holiday.

We saved for ages beforehand, after we had got permission from our folks. And as far as I was concerned, I got what nearly amounted to the Ten Commandments thrown in as well from my parents. My father:

> If yeh get tae go, then remember yeh'll no hae anybody tae bail yeh oot o' any daft nonsense, so yeh'll hiv tae watch whit yehr up tae.
>
> Yeh'll hae tae save the money fir yehr digs an yehr travel on yehr own. Then me an yehr mither'll gie yeh yehr spendin money.
>
> Nae monkey business gettin on an aff trains an boats. Yeh could get killed. (*Okay, Dad, I'll certainly try to dodge that one*).
>
> Treh an think aboot whit yehr dain, before yeh go divin' in, an no efter it! And under no circumstances do yeh go intae a pub. Hiv yeh got that?

For the benefit of those who are not quite as old as me, back when I was sixteen, most young women wouldn't have gone into a pub with their pals. Actually, most women back then only went into the pub when they were accompanied by their partners.

Lots of pubs were men-only domains. Do you know, now I'm thinking about it, some pubs used to have sawdust on the floors and spittoons. Just like the Wild West?

It was only with the advent of equality for women that pubs began to smarten up their images, and now look at some of them; you can even take your kids in for a meal. And quite right too!

So, back to my holiday Ten Commandments. My mother:

Mind an look at the bed sheets when yeh get there, tae see if thir clean, an if thir no, then jist gae an demand that somebody shifts the bed. Fir yeh'll certainly no sleep in a bed at the back o' some stranger that could hae Goad knows whit!

When yehr at the dancing stick weh yehr pals an come up the road weh them. In fact, jist stick weh yehr pals, fuhl stop.

Pose [hide] yehr money someplace in the room whaur naebody'll get it, fir Eh ken you, if yeh humph the hale lot aboot yeh'll lose it a.' An don't spend it a' in the furst twa days, fir then yeh'll be skint.

Oh! An Eh'll gie yeh tanners an coppers fir the phone. An *don't* spend them, fir yeh'll phone the phone box alang the road when yeh get there, an halfway through the week, an when yehr ready tae come hame.

Nae actin the goat at they railway stations. An on that boat tae Rothesay bide awa' fae the rails. Yeh kin droond in wahter! *(That one was to be quite prophetic in a way).*

In fact . . . nae dangerous monkeyshines at a'!

* * *

It reminded me of when I was a kid, and we were all going to some function or other, and my father would line us all up, every time, and say:

'Right! Nae runnin aboot like wild Indians an annoyin abody. Nae screamin an shoutin. Nae eatin anything that yeh've no' been offered. And remember, if yeh mak a fool o' us, yeh've tae come hame weh me. Now jist enjoy yehrsels.'

Yeh right yeh are, Father. That'll be dead easy now!

With all my holiday instructions in mind, that I could happily ignore once I was out of sight, I set about getting my holiday money together by getting a Saturday job with the SCWS where I was working at the time.

I knew that if I proved to my folks that I could indeed get the money together for my holiday (and I knew they had their doubts), then they would stick to their end of the deal and supply the spending money. I also knew that I'd get more spending money than they had promised if I managed to save up the rest.

Then they would both tell me to have a good time and mean it!

Looking back on it all now, like most teenagers, I never gave a thought to how they must feel that I was about to be let loose in another part of Scotland, and for the first time ever, stay out for more than the one night when I would be staying at my pals. And as is the way of all generations, they had to let me go and start losing the girl that had been theirs up to now, and the feelings they might have about that.

On the other hand, I may be waxing a bit lyrical here! Maybe they thought it was money well spent to get some peace and quiet for a week, and when I left the house with my bag I wasn't the only one clapping my hands silently! Maybe they were clapping their hands . . . and their feet as well!

That aside, I would imagine that 'dangerous monkeyshines' bit from my mother meant . . . boys. But when I was sixteen we were about as mature as today's' fourteen year olds, and I would have run a mile if some guy had suggested sex to me!

Just now was about getting up to some of the warned about monkeyshines, and that kept me happy. Safe in the knowledge that my parents were far too old to know anything at all, (a fact I didn't tell them) and that I could certainly look after myself!

Back then practically no one had a telephone, (much less mobiles) and folk just had to use the nearest phone box to keep in touch. My mother provided the phone money so that I had no excuses about not having change or being broke, etc. etc. So, as I departed on my holiday I was given my 'ET-phone-home orders' and the number of the phone box at the end of the road. And call home I did, because I wanted to get away on my own for more than one holiday!

It was not unknown to go to the phone box at an agreed time and, if somebody else was on the phone, to open the door and ask if they were just having a blether, as you were waiting on a call. And if they were just having a blether then most of the time they cut their phone call short to let you in.

At last, the day of the Rothesay holiday dawned. The suitcase had been checked and packed. The dookers were in there in case the sun came out. The pieces and the goodies were made up for the train, and then the boat over to Rothesay.

As I remember, the journey passed well. We were in the old style train that had carriages that held up to eight people, and you had to either get your case up on the rack, or just stick it somewhere beside you.

I would imagine that the three of us cleared out any other occupants of our carriage before we'd even crossed the old Dundee rail bridge.

Then off the train, on the boat and off the pier at glorious Rothesay!

I loved that place when I first saw it. As I remember it, it was a lovely wee place. I can't remember if it was raining but it was the West Coast of Scotland, so no doubt it was. But it had a lovely walk alongside the water and it had a Pavilion along the seafront that we discovered was the dance hall. So far so good!

Our hotel was up a hill and looked like an old Georgian Mansion. So after lugging bags and baggage up that hill in we went!

It had the typical aspidistra plant sitting on a hall table covered with a red velvet table runner. And as we entered the lady of the establishment greeted us, by getting us to sign the book and telling us the rules.

Obviously, no guests in the rooms, she emphasised. No bringing food into the rooms. Being late for meals might mean you got none (it was to prove later that we didn't anyway). No noise after a certain time, which I can't remember, but it sure wouldn't be much after eleven I would imagine. Enjoy our stay! Okey dokey! I can tell you I felt right at home! But at least I could ignore her in earnest!

So we trekked and hauled our bags up about four or five flights of stairs, right to the very top floor. The landlady showed us where the bathroom was that served the two rooms that were on our landing, then we entered an attic room that was like being back living up the West End.

There was a huge mirror above the fireplace. There were two double beds and one small single bed, all stuck in together. There was one wardrobe, and the sea view was 'seeing' the seagulls as they flew past. But ... it was spotless, for we checked the minute she left the room. And you know what? At the age I am now, I would have hated that room, but we were the age we were then, and did we care that we were all bunged in one room? No we didn't. We were there to have a good time, and that was what we intended to dedicate ourselves to.

During that week we even hung a pulley across the window and hung our underwear and stockings there to dry, without even a thought for the folk opposite, who thankfully never told the landlady, who I'm sure would've had a rule that said;

'No knickers waving about my window in plain sight of the rest of Rothesay.'

We had arrived in the morning so, after we'd dumped the luggage, we went out for our first nosey at Rothesay and all the wee shops, bought a cone and then returned for lunch and that was surprise number one.

I was brought up on mince, veggies, steak pie, dumplings and all things plain but filling. Now the food was good enough, but the portions were my wee sister's size! I can't remember properly now but I think my first lunch there was half a fish and about three chips and ten peas.

Back home even if it was just an egg with a pile of chips, my plate was always full and I could eat as much bread as I wanted. But you could have stuck your whole lunch onto a slice of bread and still had room left. And to boot, there was one slice of bread each and that was it. Then the sweet was a saucer of jelly with two mandarin segments.

In defence of Rothesay, and as I don't want to go upsetting the folk there, let me say I *know* that we were just unlucky, and it could have been any place in Dundee, or indeed Scotland, that we got mediocre digs. But we all loved Rothesay and there was a great chippie not too far away, and the fish in Rothesay almost jumped out of the water and into the chip shop!

So we immediately went on to plan B. We would ignore all her rules and start off by smuggling food in if we were hungry.

Next we went out and found out all about the dance hall and decided we'd go there that evening. And we did! We must have enjoyed that a lot because I think we went there most evenings.

However, the first night in the boarding house we agreed that since one bed looked better than the other, we'd all take turns in that.

When you think about it now, if you go to a hotel and they don't shift the towels every day *and the bed*, if you're there more than two days, then you think you're ill-done by. We never gave a thought to using the same towels for a week, or jumping in and out of different beds all week long.

By this time we were well into enjoying our holiday even though we were all lumped in together, (remember we'd all lived in tenements), and of course we were getting our first taste of true *freedom!*

I had called the Fintry phone box when I arrived the first day and my mother had picked up right away. I imagine she had killed the person who was there and told her she couldn't get the phone. 'Yes! The journey was fine. Yes! I still had my money! Yes! The digs (accommodation to those posh folk who were in Rothesay) were fine! Yes! The woman was feeding us well.' What else could I say?

You think I wanted my mother on a boat to Rothesay like it was the D-Day landings? Worse still ... she might bring my father with her, and that would really 'pit-the-ba-on-the-slatties'.

'Yes! I would call again on the agreed day and at the agreed time. Yes! I did know that she couldn't hold up the phone box and had to go, and I would have to be there next time at the exact time I was told!' And finally, 'NO! I had not got into any bother or anything else I was not telling her! Okay, I would have a good time!'

So, back to the attic at the top of the boarding house in Rothesay, at approximately eleven o'clock at night.

One of the double beds was parallel with a wall that had

a door in it. As it was my turn to sleep there that night, and as I jumped into bed, I tried the handle to see if it was locked, just in case an axe murderer was next door. Absolute silence!

So on the basis that an axe murderer would've got it sorted out by just coming through the door with his axe and seeing us off, I guess I felt it was just Joe Normal who was next door.

On thinking about it now, maybe it was some couple who'd saved up for a holiday all year, to get away to the peace and quiet of Rothesay and then landed next door to us, where the words peace and quiet meant just don't go absolutely nuts! So they'd up and moved to another room pronto!

Anyway, 'Less of the monkeyshines' as my parents would have said, didn't apply now, because Joy of Joys and Tra-la-la-Tra-lal-la-Tra-la-la they weren't here, so real life rules didn't apply.

After a spell of jumping about beds and high jinks it was decided;

'Look wid better shut up an get tae sleep afore somebody really complains!'

Never mind complain! They could've let off the one o'clock gun if we'd been standing in the ramparts of Edinburgh Castle and we wouldn't have heard it with the noise we'd been making!

So off to the Land of Nod! But what was this? The mattress on the bed was covered with huge big white buttons that were now sticking in our backs. Never mind just go to sleep! Ten minutes later . . . no way! This was now like lying on a bed of nails. So what would we do?

Then I had a brainwave! I should cut off the buttons that were sticking in our backs and then we could sew them back on again before we left and no one would be any the wiser!

In my mind's eye right now I see the look on my father's face as if he'd been there. I got out of bed, pulled back the sheet and started cutting the buttons off the woman's mattress.

I learnt then that the buttons also kept the flock *inside* the mattress, and when you cut the buttons, tiny piles of flock pushed through the holes and sewing the buttons back on ceased to be an option. And, of course, eventually the bed was knocked out of shape. But it didn't happen when we were there. Well, never mind! So what was my answer to the flock bubbling through the mattress?

I just stopped cutting buttons off the mattress immediately, hurriedly put the sheet back on, cancelled the fact that I'd cut off any buttons in the first place, and stuck the evidence (buttons) behind the mirror!

We never looked at the mattress again in case we found something we didn't want to see. And the place wouldn't be dusted until we left, so the incriminating buttons were safe as well!

When I think about it I had the hard neck to complain about this woman's' digs! However, it all landed up in trouble anyway before we left, when we were caught sneaking in fish suppers, and we told her that if she'd fed us more than would keep a spuggie (sparrow) alive, then we wouldn't have to spend our hard earned holiday money on buying extra food anyway.

And so my first holiday on my own came to an end and vanished into memories that have faded over the years.

But . . . the one, constant, remaining memory I have of Rothesay is the day that my two pals and I (we're pals to this day) decided that we would take a boat out on the sea and become sailors.

Remember here that you're talking about youngsters whose knowledge of the sea extended to Errol Flynn in his swashbuckling roles at the cinema, or getting on the Fifie boat and crossing from Dundee to Wormit, or rowing a cobble across the Swannie Ponds. But then again we were born and bred Dundonians, so why wouldn't we be able to row a boat on the open sea?

Next morning, we couldn't wait as we walked along the seafront to the docking hut where the guy who rented out the boats sat. Had we ever taken a boat out before he asked? We certainly had we answered!

So we paid our money and asked if we could leave our coats in his shed since it was a lovely sunny day and then jumped gleefully into this wee boat. Now this was being on holiday at Rothesay right enough!

One of my pals sat in the bow beside the rudder, my other pal and I sat and took up our oars and, as Long John Silver would've said: 'Avast, me hearties, cast off and let's be shot of this infernal shore!' And so we did!

Oh, the bliss of life on the open waves! I can remember loving rowing away in this boat of ours. My pal, who was steering and being the captain, was doing a better job than Jim Hawkins from *Treasure Island*. We were young, we were free and we were at sea!

Then . . . we passed by this metal triangle on a pole that was painted bright red and stuck out of the water:

'What's that?' asked the Captain.

'What?' The oarsmen looked at the red triangle!

'Oh!' said the Oarsman called Mae, who knew all about the sea because she'd watched so many films about sea things. 'That'll be fir anchorin yehr boat if yeh want tae hae a break fae the rowin!'' said she, with the absolute conviction of one who knows absolutely zilch about sea things!

'Oh! Right yeh are,' said the rest of the crew, who knew as much as she did.

'Well we're no wantin a break are weh?' asked the Captain?

'No!' agreed the rest of the crew. And so we buccaneers continued to row, outwards and onwards, ever outwards and onwards, into the beautiful blue sea.

Suddenly our peace was shattered!

A distant whistle sounded from the shore, blowing over and over again. We looked round in the direction of the noise and there was the boatman with his yellow waterproof jacket, jumping up and down and waving his hands. He was by this time so small that he looked liked a demented wee canary on a bit of elastic.

'Whit's up weh him?'

It's no time tae come back in yet?'

'Jist ignore him.'

So we returned to look at the beautiful blue ocean, just in time to see . . . a bloody great big Rothesay Steamer heading what looked like straight towards us and was practically on our doorstep!

Did we stay calm in the face of this adversity? You bet we didn't! That *really* only happens in the movies!

We started rowing like galley slaves that were about to be battered with the leather cat-o-nine tails. I panicked and promptly lost my oar, so we started going round in circles, as my pal rowed furiously but going nowhere!

The wash off the Rothesay Steamer (that, thank goodness, was actually quite a bit away) came towards us, shot us up in the air and down again and we promptly lost the other oar.

So now we couldn't row at all. But at least that big daft boat had moved towards the shore and away from us!

The wee yellow canary man had vanished, either fainted or deid, and we were now adrift.

See when you see Charlton Heston in that religious movie, just lying on that raft and dying quietly, well I say, good for him! For we started yelling loud enough that you could've heard us in Davie Jones' Locker.

Harsh reality was now telling us that we had no way of getting back.

Then, huge sighs of relief. We spotted them.

Our heroes floated nearby in a motor boat. So it was a bit like a movie, I suppose. And it proves my theory that there is almost always a Good Samaritan there when you need one. Or put it another way, the Devil looks after his own!

These three guys had been out on the water in this motor boat and had seen what happened, so they scooted on over and threw us a wee grappling hook tied on the end of a rope, which we hooked into our boat and they started to tow us in to shore.

Then something else dawned on us! We'd only gone and lost wee canary man's oars! So how would we face him!

Reply! We didn't! I shouted over to our rescuers;

'Could yeh tow us tae anither bit o' the beach cause wiv lost the guys oars, an wir no wantin tae go back there an face him?'

'No problem!'

So our gallant rescuers dropped us off at another cove in the beach and said they would let the man know where his boat was. I don't remember ever speaking to them in the dancing or any place else after that. So they will forever be our anonymous heroes.

We, by this time, had recovered from our 'weh-nearly-got-droond drama' and now that our feet were back on dry land, we were having a great laugh about all this, when one of my pals stopped dead:

'Hey! Heez still got oor coats!'

Were we about to go and ask for our coats back? Well what do you think?

* * *

I have a photo that shows the three of us in Rothesay, standing at the railings, with the ocean behind us, which I call in my heart 'The Dundee sailors'. And it also reminds me of what it was to be that young and foolish! Although I still try to manage and pack in a few '*Yeh niver gone an done that, hiv yeh?*' just to keep me on my toes!

* * *

When I arrived home safe and sound from my first ever adult holiday, and after I had dished out the usual wee jewellery boxes made out of shells and the bookmarks with Rothesay on them, and the special paperweight with a boat on it that I had bought for my mother, I had, of course, to tell everybody about my adventures.

It will surprise no one reading this I would imagine, that none of us related our boating trip to anyone until much later on.

We maybe weren't much catch as sailors, but we were never daft!

Now if this had been written in 1956 or 1957 and canary man had read it, I can just hear him saying:

'So that's the daft young buggars that lost my oars and had me dragging the boat back from God knows where along the shore. I remember them alright!'

And, I bet he just binned our coats!

8

THE BOUGHT HOOSE

My early childhood may have been spent up the West End of Dundee, but my proper growing up took place in Fintry housing scheme in the 1950s and 1960s. We had moved to our second (bigger) house in Fintry with its own up and downstairs.

My older brother had married and now had a place of his own.

My elder sister was also married and was back living up the West End, but she and my brother-in-law had decided they wanted to buy their own house. This in itself was quite a 'big' thing to do, as far as we were all concerned.

Things were changing, economically and culturally. The working class was earning more money, folk had more disposable income so, of course, lending institutions and banks were opening up their doors to folk they wouldn't have given a nod to back in my mother's time.

I remember my mother telling me that when she was young, if someone had a bank book they were considered well off! In the main, her generation rented where they lived and wouldn't even have entertained the thought of buying a house.

As my sister's house was being built, I can remember going down with her sometimes and watching that house go up from just bricks, and I couldn't wait for it to be finished so that I could visit her!

When things were a few months from completion my sister and my brother-in-law came to live with us for a short spell, until they could move into their own house. So we just all got re-arranged.

My younger brother was relegated to sleeping in the dinette so they could have his room. Yes, we had a dinette by then and 'loabies' were turning into halls. But remember my brother used to sleep in a chairbed when he was really wee and seven of us lived in two tiny rooms up the West End. So, he managed in the dinette just fine!

I was now sharing 'the lassies room' with my younger sister.

Now, here we were, back to seven of us in one house.

The difference this time being that seven of us in one house, when I was wee, meant a two-roomed, low door flat in a tenement, with an outside toilet up the close. So it wasn't any real hardship at all for seven of us to be in a three-bedroomed house with its own dinette!

Do you know I'd have thought I was a real toff from the Sinderens if someone had said to me when I was a kid that I'd live in a house with a dinette? The kitchen in my house up the West End was so small that when we all sat down to have a meal, two of us sat on the bed that was housed in the bed recess, while the rest of my family sat round the gate-leg table that folded down when it was not in use.

I can remember when the table was out full-sized, my mother could lean over from the table and lift the teapot from the top of the cooker if she wanted another cup of tea.

Now we had two rooms for eating in, but we still all ate in the kitchen (I still like eating in the kitchen best). The dinette was mainly reserved for visitors, when the polished table with its under felt and a linen tablecloth with flowers embroidered on it, would be trotted out. And the china cups and saucers would get an airing as well.

* * *

That reminds me of a story my brother-in-law tells about the first time he came to our house when he and my sister were 'serious', and she was bringing him up to meet 'the femily'.

He recalls sitting in the living room talking to my father as my mother was away in the kitchen 'seeing to the tea'.

We all wandered in one at a time to have a look at him, and I bet he felt like he was on parade by the time we'd all had a butchers. Although if memory serves me, I think my father did all the 'conversationing'.

My logic was that it was better to say little than to say the wrong thing the first time '*meh sister's lad*' was visiting.

There was a wooden food hatch between our kitchen and the living room, which was handy, but it was handiest of all at meal times when the food was ready. My mother would bang on the hatch with the end of a knife and bellow something like; 'TEA's UP!' Then we all knew that was the signal to come and get it!

So my brother-in-law was sitting there, making polite conversation with my dad, when this *batter-batter-batter* rattles off the hatch and we all vanish, leaving him and my dad to bring up the rear.

By the time he got through the room we were all sitting down and raring to go. He always says we left that room like we'd been fired from a cannon!

Then, there was the occasion when there was only my older sister, my prospective brother-in-law and me in the house, and we were having chips with our tea. My sister left me for five minutes to look after the chips 'an no let them burn'.

Well, as I'd watched my mother, the 'chip' expert, since I was a kid, I decided to 'shake' the pan like my mother did to make sure all the chips cooked evenly. I gave the chip pan a couple of almighty 'shoogles', and the hot fat slopped over the side of the pan, and right on to the naked flame of the gas ring it was sitting on!

There was this whoosh as the fat caught fire and snaked its way across the cooker like a mini mill fire!

I let out a yell:

'Eh've set the chip pan up! Eh've set the chip pan up!'

My prospective brother-in-law came flying through the room, as my sister rushed back down the stairs and opened the back door. He threw a dishtowel over the chip pan and bunged it out into the back green! And that was another crisis diverted.

If memory serves me, my sister was (yet again) less pleased with me that the tea was ruined and that there had been an uproar.

I remember thinking (yet again) *That's the last time Eh'm gonna help her!* But on the other hand, I *had* learned not to shake a chip pan so vigorously.

So, anyway, they both came back to stay with us until they could move into their new house that was being built specially for them! We thought that was great!

And it was on one really cold wintry day while they were staying with us that one of my favourite memories of that time, that I shared with my young sister, happened.

The entrance to our front door was preceded by six steps

that led on to a path, then a step up to a stone-clad veranda (yes would you believe it; we had a veranda *and* a dinette *and* a hall and a food hatch (talk about 'à la posh').

Now that we were all older, my mother was back working part-time in the mills in the mornings. I think she had originally gone back to save up for my older sister's wedding, but the money had come in handy, so she'd just decided to stay on.

She was always first away to work in the mornings and my brother-in-law had an early start as well.

So, at about 6.30 a.m., my mother wakened us up with a, 'Wir aff! Dinna sleep in!' bellowed up from the hall, accompanied by us hearing my father in the next door room muttering out loud:

'Thir's somebody died fower bliddy streets awa that yeh've no managed tae get up!' as my mother banged the door shut and departed!

My young sister and I just lay there trying to ignore the early morning wake up, when a minute later the peace was broken yet again with a shout from outside of, '*WOOOAHHH! OH! MEH GOAD!*'

My sister and I jumped up, knelt up on the bed (which was over at the window that looked out over our path); pulled back the curtains and were greeted by a snowy white, frosty, street.

Now, my brother-in-law cycled to his work and he'd his bike over his shoulder until he got to the road. But the path was covered with invisible black ice, so he started to slither right down the path and onto the stairs.

My mother also took off and went skating at the back of him, grabbed the back wheel of his bike to save herself, sent them both off their balance in earnest; and they landed in a heap at the bottom of the stairs!

After we had made sure they were alright, my sister and I fell back on the bed in silent laughter. It was just like a Charlie Chaplin film! And the best was yet to come!

My mother and brother-in-law just got up and shook themselves down, and I could hear my mother laughing, but neither of them came back to 'salt down' the path. My sister waited until they were out of sight, and said to me, 'Maybe we should tell Dad?'

But we didn't!

My father was next to leave and by this time we were on ear alert. Next thing we heard was; 'Skid! Skitter! Skid! BUMP!' accompanied by at least two machine-gun rattled 'J***S C*****S!'

We dived up and peered through the curtains. His bunnet had gone one way, his fag had gone another, whilst he and his peices (I know, it should be sandwiches for folk that have dinettes and food hatches) went the other.

My father, who was always aware of his dignity, got up as quick as a flash, dusted down his bunnet, lit up another fag and then went off muttering 'Good gracious me', or words to that effect! And *he* didn't come back and salt the path either! I thought we were going to burst a gasket over that little scenario!

The last one out before us was my older sister. So out she goes! By this time we were up at that window before she'd even shut the door! And ups-a-daisy, off she went! But I have to say that she went down like a ballet dancer; she just sloped over to the side and slid graciously to the ground.

It must've been near Christmas for she'd a whole load of envelopes all over the place. This time we fell back on the bed and howled out loud, for there was no one to hear us but my young brother, who'd immediately leapt out of bed when he'd heard my sister and gone to help her!

I did, however, salt the entire path down before we set foot on it!

Now! I have no idea who told my father that we had been privy to all this early morning slap-stick (I guess I must've let the cat out of the bag as usual), but I *can* tell you that my young sister and I were treated to a *'Naebody kin beat oor father'* dressing down on the fact that someone might have really been hurt, and we'd thought it was some kind of a joke!

Not being completely daft, we said nothing and looked as remorseful as we could until we got back in everybody's good books. We also refrained from pointing out to my father that none of *them* had come back to salt the path so that *we* might not have an accident, because we *did* know (with my father), when to keep our mouths *shut!*

My sister and I still have laugh about that escapade to this day.

Anyway, after the 'Charlie Chaplin on ice day', a packet of salt was left in the hall behind the front door and whoever was out first in the frosty mornings after that, or whoever noticed the path was icy (meaning us), 'went an pit saht on the path'.

In due course, the day arrived when my sister and her husband moved into their 'new hoose'. It was really lovely, and they were delighted, and we were delighted for them.

Our house reverted back to normal. My young brother got his room back and we all settled back in, at least for a wee while, until future life events changed our 'normal' yet again!

Oh, and the dinette went back to being itself!

9

AULD KINDS O' NEW YEARS

In the 1950s and 1960s, it wasn't only kids who played party games on high days and holidays. At New Year, lots of folk held New Year parties and played party games! New Year celebrations back then were totally different animals from what they are today. For a kick-off, Hogmanay was just as big a day as Christmas Day, and celebrated every bit as much, mainly because Christmas wasn't nearly so commercialised at that time, and getting 'a present' meant just that. You got one big present and then just a load of wee diddles and some goodies.

So, after all the cleaning and running around that was necessary for Christmas Day ended on 25th December, my mother would draw breath, tidy up on the 26th, and then guess what? On the 27th, it would start all over again for Hogmanay.

The butcher's order that had been reserved would be collected; including another huge steak pie, (we usually had a butcher's steak pie on Christmas Day as well).

My father was in charge of the drink so he'd be seeing to that.

By the time we were all growing up in Fintry, however,

my mother had her own wee army and we'd all to muck in. By the time Hogmanay arrived, the Health Authorities could've visited my house, and if they'd found an item of dirty clothing, or a loose speck of dust, I'd have eaten my hat!

Also, by the time I was in my teens, the spontaneity of just 'dropping in' on each other's houses after the 12 o'clock bells was becoming much more difficult. Mainly because the huge exodus to the housing schemes forced folk to live much further apart.

What became increasingly popular were weekend parties that were organised for weeks after Hogmanay, so that friends and families could have a get together.

But no matter how far away folk lived, we (my pals and I) just set our plans for after the dancing came out on Hogmanay, and we walked the distances that were required. Sometimes we would all 'bunce' (pay equal shares) for a taxi, but the norm was Shanks Pony!

The biggest half of Dundee who intended to go first-footing usually met up in the City Square to see in the New Year, and then departed to wherever. We would walk a planned route and visit all the various houses on the way to the last visit. This could take up most of the night and continue into the early hours of the morning.

But even if you were with just your pals (pals were always girls back then), there were so many folk out and about for the whole night that you felt perfectly safe, and you would never have dreamt of walking past anyone without wishing them 'Happy New Year!' and receiving back, 'Eh! An a Happy New year tae you ana.'

When I was a kid, I used to sing this wee song at New Year time: 'A happy new year, a bottle o' bear, an a skelp in the ja' fir next New Year.' Obviously, that one was a throw back from the Stone Age when walloping each other was a way of saying hello!

When I got older there could be a drawback to all this camaraderie, which was the kissing of strangers. Some guys saw it as a chance to just enjoy themselves, and if they looked like they'd had one too many as they zoomed in, I'd do a quick whip round and presented the side of my face. Other than that though, I just enjoyed myself along with the rest of them.

After the dancing was over we would make for the City Square. The intention was to reach there about 11:30 p.m. The Overgate, Reform Street and along the High Street would be bursting at the seams. At the witching hour, the old Steeple clock would strike twelve. A rocket would zoom off from the roof of the Caird Hall, there would be a great cheer from the crowds and we'd all sing 'Auld Lang Syne', and go bananas for about fifteen minutes.

Men would take out their New Year bottle and you'd pass the 'bottle' around your own wee crowd first. No guy would have dreamt of turning up at the Square without a bottle, even the non-drinkers. All the lads had to have a bottle to toast in the New Year whether you took a drink from any of the bottles or not.

As I remember not many of us girls took a drink of whisky. Or maybe that's just me, for I never could stand the smell of whisky!

By the time I was old enough to go first-footing we went to the Palais in Tay Street. At Hogmanay, most of the dance halls had cloakrooms where the lads had to put their bottle and they got a 'bottle ticket', for you weren't allowed drink inside that dance hall (like that stopped them). So you can imagine the mad rush for coats and bottles that took place at 11 p.m. when it was time for the Palais to close.

The big sparkly swirly ball that was suspended from the roof of the Palais sparkled over an empty dance floor when the last dance was being played. We were with the other revellers struggling through the melee in the cloakrooms, so that we'd be at the Square in time.

Armed to the teeth with all our Hogmanay necessities, we'd march down the old Overgate, saying hello to anyone we knew. There were stalls all over the place, out on the streets selling first-foots.

Smoked herrings hung around in their hundreds, dressed up in their fancy multi-coloured crêpe dresses. I have yet to find out what that was all about, but never in my puff would I have stuck a 'deid fish' in my handbag!

You could also buy wee first-footing gifts all wrapped up in nice paper; lumps of shiny new coal (haven't a clue what that was about either) ... in fact, you could almost buy anything you liked because the shops were all open as well!

I always bought my own first-footing gifts beforehand and carried them with me in a bag that also held the high heels you'd worn to the dancing. Since it was Dundee, Scotland, you lived in, and you were to be jaunting in and out of houses for hours, socks and boots were the order of the day. But when you got to the houses you always kicked your boots off in the 'loabies' (halls now) and put on you high heels.

Oh! Here's something that happened to one of my high heels in a house I landed up in one New Year.

The man of the house said that he had this game we would all enjoy! Everyone would throw their right shoe in the middle of the floor, we'd all to go out onto the 'plehtie' (outside walkway; he was three stairs up in a tenement), then he'd mix up all the shoes, put out all the lights and we'd all to come back into the house and find our own shoe in the dark! Seemed like good fun, so we all trooped out onto the 'plehtie' like a bunch of lemmings, leaving all our shoes in a great big heap in the middle of his floor! After a wee while this guy bellows:

'Right yeh are lads! Ready or nut! Come in an find yehr shoes!'

Now the 'man o the hoose'; in his infinite wisdom, when he got us all out of the way, just took all our shoes, opened the window and scattered the shoes to the four winds and down into the back green below.

Once we were all back into the darkened room, he switched on the lights, pointed to the open window and said:

'This is the best buht o' the geme. Yehr shoes are a' doon in the back greenie.' And then he nearly split his sides laughing!

Do you know what? I can't recall anyone even getting angry. We just all dashed down to the greenie and dived about looking for our shoes. I was lucky that I had boots sitting in his hall, so at least my feet were dry. What about the folk that only had one shoe on?

One guy's shoe landed on top of the roof of some old washie shed in the back greenie, and he'd to scramble up though the snow and slush to get it back! Right enough! I bet he was none too happy with 'mine host!'

The shoes I had on that year were sparkly, black suede, sling-back high heels (that I'd saved up for), and if you've ever seen a fragile black suede shoe that's been bunged the length of a three-storey tenement, landed in the snow and slush, and *then* been tramped over in the pitch-black by as many feet (some of them size tens) looking for their own shoe, then you'll know why my New Year's shoes that year were relegated from split-new to no-sae-new in the space of twenty-four hours!

Oh, and another Hogmanay, I landed up getting evicted from a house because one of the visitors (not anyone I was with I hasten to add, *and that's the truth*) had felt cold and decided to 'poker up' the woman's fire. Only thing was . . . it was one of the fancy new electric ones with an orange-coloured light bulb and a metal spinner behind imitation *coal!*

So the woman's new posh fire was wrecked, which I bet she'd saved up for for ages! Or worse still, had taken it out on a M'Gills line and it would still have to be payed for! Hence, the lady of the house was so upset that she just up and told everybody who was there at the time to go (or words to that effect)!

Anyway . . . back to Hogmanay in the centre of Dundee!

At the bottom of the Overgate, just across from where Boots is now, there used to be a huge caravan that sold sausages on a roll, mince on a roll, chips, hot dogs, meat pies ('pehs' to us) and steak bridies *(Eh'll hae a plehn ane, an an ingin ane ana)*. He even did big slices of fried dumpling! Drink may have not been my thing, but there's never been anything wrong with my appetite. It was food for the gods indeed, or the Dundee reveller!

This van sat at the bottom of the Overgate every week-end, but on Hogmanay that caravan mannie must have been clapping his feet, never mind his hands, for the money he made. And when I think on it, there I'd be all dolled up to the nines in my New Year's outfit, stuffing my face with a mince roll or a bridie. It would have tasted orgasmic if I'd known what that meant back then! And it's a good job my mother or father won't be reading that last sentence!

When I was 'oot furst-fuhttin' and had reached my own

home, that was usually my last port of call. When I got in my mother would give me a great big hug accompanied by:

'Happy New Year, an many o them! Did yeh enjoy yersel? Did athin go okay?'

Reassured that I'd had a great time, and yes everything went absolutely fine, she ushered us into the living room to join whoever was at my house.

Now if I'd brought a crowd with me the first thing my father did was see who needed a drink. Apart from me that is! My father would never offer us (his own family) what he called 'hard drink!' I could have a sherry or a cordial, but he wouldn't have liked it if I'd asked for anything else. The whole room could have got 'stoatin' as long as it wasn't me.

That never bothered me one hoot! And even in later years, if we had a family 'night oot' or were at a dance and my parents were there I would get myself a drink if I wanted to, but always drowned it with something else so it was in a big glass. They were happy with all that kid-olgy, so it was never any big deal to me.

* * *

When we lived in Fintry my parents always organised a Saturday New Year's party sometime soon after Hogmanay. All our friends did the same thing. These Saturday parties could go on for weeks, because most of the folk that came to our 'do' had one as well.

My mother always jumped in as quickly as she could so that our party was over and done. She did this because:

Beh the time February's here, an Annie Lawrie's died fir the hundredth time, or wir stull devin aboot weh perty gemes, eh'm quite happy tae dae that in somebody else's hoose, but Eh like meh hoose back in oarder beh the end o the furst month!

So, on our allotted Saturday, it was up at the crack of dawn for everybody! My mother would prepare all the food: a huge steak pie; a casserole full of sausages and onions; a pot of mince; a huge pot of soup (always my favourite); an absolutely massive ashet of mashed potatoes; and, of course, sausage rolls. But there was no buffet-sized anything back then. My mother used to buy a load of big sausage rolls from the butcher and cut them up. To follow there was the inevitable clootie dumpling, shortie and bun. Between that and the drink no wonder some folk landed up 'praying to shanks' after they'd been to one of the New Year Saturday 'dos'.

I recall coming home quite late once to one of my parents' parties, after I'd been away with my pals doing some after-Hogmanay partying of our own. When I came in our house was bursting at the seams. I think the world and his wife had turned up. So I decided to retreat to the kitchen to get something to eat and here's this guy I'd never seen before, standing over the cooker doing himself a 'fry-up'. He looked round at me as I sat down at the table:

'Hi there.'

'Hi.'

'If yehr wantin somethin, help yehrsel! That's whit the wummin o' the hoose jist telt me tae come ben an dae. Jist eat anythin Eh wanted. So Eh thought Eh'd dae a freh-up! Dae yeh want some?'

'Na! Yehr fine thanks! Eh'll jist hae some soup.'

We both served ourselves and sat down at my kitchen table.

'Whaur dae you live?' says He.

'Here,' I replied.

He just looked at me for a moment:

'Oh, good. You'll ken whaur the HP sass is then, dae yeh?'

I remember having a conversation with my mother in later years about the HP sauce episode, and the fact that back then folk *were* able to leave their doors open. These things were our normal, and what had happened from then to now? She replied:

Fowk are fowk, an 99% o' them are stull trehin the best they kin manage fir thirsels an thir bairns.

An anither thing! Half that's sade aboot the guid auld days is jist a load o tripe! Eh've tae laugh when aulder ains wax lyrical about life bein a lot better then! Well they niver lived up meh street that's fir sure!

Gie me a purse that's aye got some money in it, meh hoover, meh washin machine, an meh central heatin any day!

An the reason yeh kid aye leave yehr doors open wiz thir *wiz buggar all tae steal* . . . apert fae bairns; an abody hid enough o' them thirsel!

Then she would say:

But Eh do think that whit weh definitely did hae, wiz ane anither, a sense of belangin, an no jist tae yehr ain family, but tae hundreds jist like yeh! An yeh niver felt yeh wir in it on yehr own! We knew wha's side weh wir on! An that's ane o' the biggest losses fir the young anes now, as far as Eh kin tell!

Anyway, back to our parties in the 1950s.

As well as the dancing and the singing, there was a variety of party games:

Birl the Bottle

Everyone found a chair, or pulled up a bit of the carpet, and an empty lemonade or drink bottle was spun on the carpet, in the middle of the floor.

When it stopped spinning the person that the neck of the bottle was pointing towards had to sing a song.

That was when the, 'Oh-no-dinna-ask-me-tae-gie-a-sang' brigade headed for the kitchen to eat and have a blether, and the rest of us had a good old sing-a-long! I'd been joining in sing-songs from since I can remember what singing was all about. I'd heard all the old Irish songs about banishment to the colonies, some sojer's died on a battlefield and so on. I'd heard my granny, grandad, uncle, auntie, best pal that's no here any mair songs, so many times before, that I knew every word off by heart. And I still do!

Birl the Bottle was usually played in between the more strenuous games and dances.

The Ferris Wheel

All the men had to take off their shoes, sit on the floor and make a circle, with their feet pointing inwards, leaving a small circle in the middle of the ring. The women had to take their shoes off and go and stand in the circle and somebody would shout 'GO!' And the girls would throw themselves backwards onto all the outstretched hands that had to catch them, and then they would be whirled round the circle for whatever length of time was deemed necessary.

Sounds simple until you think that if anybody who was supporting the 'birlee' just dropped their arms down, then you landed in a heap! This was obviously the whole point of the game anyway!

The Lochee Tramcar

I absolutely loved this game. Once again it was shoes-off time! The folk that were to be the tramcar were selected by 'mine hosts'.

They had to sit on the floor and place their legs together straight out in front of themselves. The pattern would be man, woman and so on. His feet would point one way and hers the other. They did this until about twelve or fourteen folk had formed 'The Lochee Tramcar'.

Now here's the good bit . . . the folk that wanted a 'hurl on the tramcar' (that word 'hurl' was really appropriate) had to do a somersault over all the outstretched legs, from one end of the tramcar to the other. And if they got stuck somebody just up and shoved them on their way! Yes they did! I've seen some sights 'hurlin doon' that Lochee Tramcar I can tell you!

If you've never seen a load of folk all trying to somersault ('Tummel-cap-ma' as we would have said in my neck of the woods) over a load of legs in the middle of a room, you've never lived! I used to just about die laughing at some of the antics.

Nelson's Eye

This was a quiet wee game that I think was played to let folk get their breath back. It was a ladies-only game, and only if you'd *never* played it before did you have to take a turn.

All the women who would be taking a turn would be banished out of the room.

My father would get a kitchen chair, an old scarf for

a blindfold and a tomato cut in half with the insides all mushed up. The first victim would be blindfolded outside the room and then led in and sat on the chair in the middle of the room, and then he'd ask:

'Yeh ken wha Nelson wiz?'

'Eh.'

Did yeh ken that they wir sellin aff souvenirs fae the battle o Trafalgar?'

'No!'

'Well hud oot yehr hand, an the geme is yeh've tae guess whit Eh bought.'

The victim would hold out her hand, my father would grab a finger, shove the girl's finger into the half cut tomato and say:

'Eh bought eez bad eye!'

You should have seen some of the reactions!

All Change Seats

The girl had to pick a partner whose knee they would sit on. Once everyone had a partner my father would get a dishtowel and tie a knot in the end. He'd be blindfolded and stand in the middle of the room. The music would be put on.

Somebody was in charge of lifting the needle of the record at intervals of their own choosing, and then off we'd go. The music would go off, my father would shout 'ALL CHANGE.' With that all the guys had to change seats and all the women had to get a new lap partner. Meanwhile, my father's swinging this dishtowel, and if you got hit with the towel you were out!

It was like the charge of the Light Brigade! I've seen chairs, people and all, landing in a heap just to get away from that dishtowel.

King Spot

I think this was my *very* favourite, but not for the reason that I thought it was a brilliant game, only because my father usually got landed organising this one, after he'd had a few drinks (him and the rest of the house). Now my father was not a drinker, so he never needed a lot to make him tipsy, and that was my true enjoyment of the whole thing.

He would get an old boot polish tin and fill it with soot from the chimney, and a wee bit wet sponge. Then we'd all to sit in a chair once again (some of which belonged to the woman next door, and maybe even the next door to her, depending on our house full) or just pull up a bit of the carpet.

We would each be given a number and he'd stand in the middle of the floor and say:

'My name is King Spot and I have no spots. How many spots does number 13 have?'

If number 13 didn't answer straightaway, my father would jump in with, 'Far too slow. Far too slow,' and stick a great big spot of soot on their face!

Now number 13 had to remember that they had *one* spot, because if they said when it was their turn again: '*Number 13 has no spots*' when they did have a spot, then they got another one.

This continued until the whole room couldn't remember how many spots they had and they all landed up looking like they had the Black Death.

But the bit I liked the best was, as well as trying to get as many other numbered faces with loads of spots, you could also say:

'Number 27 has three spots how many spots has *King Spot?*'

And if my father couldn't remember or was too slow, then he got a spot as well! So, of course ,the whole room kept bouncing the question back to King Spot!

Oh, the other thing you weren't allowed to do was hesitate. You got another spot for that as well.

I have seen my father looking like a dog from *One Hundred and One Dalmatians* and that tickled me pink! Even his baldie heid was covered with spots.

My father went bald quite young, and he always said that it was our (and my mother's fault). To which my mother would reply:

'If that wiz the case Eh'd hae been baldie heided fae aboot fevhe meenits efter Eh met you!' Ah! Love! Does it not just do your heart good?

King Spot over, my mother would go round with damp dishtowels for everybody, and we just wiped the spots into streaks and got on with the party.

* * *

As I recall some of these antics it strikes me, not for the first time, how much more of a simple a life we led. There was absolutely no sophistication in any of these games, but you know what? Simple they may have been, but boy did we enjoy ourselves and have a lot of laughs, and fifty-odd years later, I'm still getting the benefit of all the memories.

Or as my mother would've said after all the revellers had departed that night/morning:

'Well . . . that perty wiz well worth the money an the butcher's bill!'

The other thing that strikes me is that everybody, young and old, were *all* included in most of these antics. The kids joined in until they were carried upstairs to sleep in one of our beds until it was time for them to go home. I would bring my pals along after wherever we'd been, and we joined in. My brothers and sisters did the same. Then there were the neighbours and our parents' pals. And anybody else that any of them decided to drag along with them!

My mother must've made that party food turn into the 'loafs and the fishes' for she always seemed to have plenty to go round.

I'd like to finish off this bit on New Year's parties with a song, as that seems to be quite appropriate to me. But it's not 'meh sang', it's 'meh dad's sang.'

My mother had a beautiful voice, and could sing like a 'lintie', and did! Even at her eightieth birthday party we could not get her away from the mike.

My father, by comparison, could not sing a note in tune, but when 'Birl the Bottle' was on the go, there was no escape for him if the party was in our house, because if it was your house, then you *had* to sing.

Sometimes you got off by doing some kind of a forfeit if you wouldn't sing. For example, go to the house about ten doors away, and ask for fried black pudding on a bread roll, or something equally as daft. Although I've been in my house one New Year when someone came back eating a fried egg roll he'd got from a house somewhere along the street!

Now, my father's sense of dignity would never have allowed him to anything like that to save himself, so he was always one of the 'Oh-no-dinna-ask-me-tae-gie-a-sang' if he was in other folks' houses, but there was no escape in his own house, so if the bottle sought him out, and it came to his turn to sing he would always say;

'Well Eh'm tellin yeh! Yeh'll be sorry yeh asked, fir Eh canna sing a note!'

To which my mother usually added, 'An eez no kiddin! Yeh *wull* be sorry!' But if 'they' insisted, he would say:

'Okay! Be it on yehr own head. Mind yeh asked fir this!'

Then he would proceed to sing the same song *every* time.

Now, I know this is paper and not a CD (or gramophone if you were at our party), but if you just imagine one of these diddling songs that went like:

'Diddley-dy-dee-dy. Diddley-dy-de-dy-de-dy-de-dy.
 Da-dy-de-dy-de-dy-de-dy-de-diddlly-dy-dy-dy!'

Then just sing that chorus over and over again. Give it a try, you'll get the idea.

Right then! Quick cough! Here we go with my father's one and only party song, straight from its roaring success, in my house in Fintry, one Saturday night sometime in January, 19-Oatcake.

Mag Gow skinned the cow
An Buddie bylt the herrin Oh!
The auld wife, she mashed the tea
An the monkey minds the bairn Oh!
Hy-dy-diddley-dy . . . Hy-dy-meh-Daddy Oh! . . .
    Hy-dy-diddley-dy
WULL NO DRINK . . . NAE MAIR . . . WHISKY . . .
    OHHHH!!

Cue thunderous applause!

Now, if I know Dundee, somebody reading the words of that song is thinking right now:

'Hey Mag Gow wiz meh grannies pal! An meh mither hid an uncle crehed Buddie!

'Oh! An Eh think the man up the road fae us whaur Eh yazed tae bide hid a monkey.

'An Eh bet **Eh** could be that bairn!'

10

SPARKLY EYES AN HEGH-HEELED SHOES

Thinking about Auld New Years I was reminded of two 'Hogmanay events' that happened to me. There were, of course, more, but these are two of my favourites.

Hogmanay Event Number One
I was about seventeen and this Hogmanay was a really big night for me!

I was getting ready to go out with my pals to the dancing, then first-footing and then back home to Fintry. I had arrived at freedom's door in earnest! I was in my element and intended to push the boat out big style!

I had bought this emerald-green satin blouse and emerald-green sparkly eyeshadow to go with it. I thought I was a right toff and at least you wouldn't miss me in the dark!

However, as I was getting ready I noticed a wee bottle of bright green sparkly dust that my wee sister had been using for making up her Christmas cards. Now this stuff had glue in it and it was luminous, so if I put that on I certainly would stand out in the crowd.

So I did just that. I pressed this green sparkle dust onto

my eyelids, right up to my eyebrows. Then, for good measure, I stuck it on to my lips as well.

I looked in the mirror and the finished results were astounding indeed! Back in those days I had auburn hair, so as far as I was concerned, I was THE BIZ!

As I darted downstairs to go out I recall my mother doing a double take and saying something along the lines of;

'In the name o' fortune . . . Hiv you hid a right look in a mirror?'

But I just laughed, promised I would be back home not too long after the bells, and shouted through the living room door a cheerio to my father. If the look on my mother's face was anything to go by, then I could well do without his comments. I might even be made to take it all off. So I just dived out the door pronto, and went off to the dancing with my pals.

We'd not long been in the dancing, and the night was going well. There seemed to be plenty of talent out that Hogmanay night!

Then it started. Not a lot at first, just a wee itch, which rapidly got worse. My eyes and lips began to swell, and the itch turned into the 'scratch-me-or-gae-aff-yehr-heid' kind.

By the time I got to the ladies' toilet to assess the damage, my pal's eyes were almost bigger than mine. I say almost, for now I looked like Kermit the frog.

My eyes were swelling up so much I could hardly see through them. My lips had followed suit, and if we'd known what collagen was back then, you'd have thought I'd just had a double dose of that!

So I tried to get it off. I splashed water from the tap. I spat on my hankie and started to rub. Not a good idea! The dreaded green lurgie held fast. The particles had glued in solid and rubbing only made it all the more sore. I was starting to look like a pal of that guy from *Horrors of the Black Museum* and, of course, the night was over for me before it had even started.

As I was sitting on the bus going home I could see folk looking in my direction as though something out the bus window on my side was really interesting. But considering it was pitch dark by this time and I could see my reflection in the bus window, I knew what they were all staring at.

The bus conductor just said, 'Fare please', gave me my ticket and walked off. It wasn't the last bus so I'm sure he was expecting much worse to come. At least I wasn't drunk or making trouble, so why should he care if I looked like a walking accident? He'd the rest of the night to get through!

I arrived home and had this thought of just letting myself in quietly, and nipping upstairs to see if I had some cream that would remove the green sparkle.

By now my whole face was beginning to ache and I knew I was going to need my mother's help. Anyway, the minute my key went in the door she appeared like the proverbial bloodhound (I'm sure she could smell when something was wrong with any of us).

She opened the kitchen door:

'Yehr back? Yehr early? Whit's happe . . . Oh, meh goad!'

My father shot out the living room like 'Oh meh goad' were the magic words calling the genie out of his bottle! He was silent for a nanosecond:

'Whit the hell hiv yeh done tae yehr face.'

'Oh meh Goad! Whit a *mess!* Yehr like yeh've jist gone ten roonds weh Joe Louis!' *(Kind words of reassurance from my mother)*.

'Eh canna help it!' *(Me on the verge of tears)* 'It's that sparkly stuff that yeh stick on the Christmas cairds! It jist stuck like glue!'

My father could see his peaceful run up to the 'bells' vanishing into the mists:

It is bliddy glue! Whit the hell possessed yeh tae dae a thing like that tae yersel? If somebody hid held yeh doon an shoved that stuff on yehr face, we'd be gettin the cruelty tae them; or worse! But yeh jist up an did it tae yersel! Well done! Ten oot o' ten fir wha kin be the daftest!

By this time, my mother had recovered enough to see that my father's blood pressure was about to go through the roof . . . and me with it, by the look of things:

'Right! Thir's nae yaze gettin in a panic!' *(Too late in my case)* 'Get up the stairs an eh'll see whit Eh kin riddle up tae treh an get it aff!'

I should explain that 'riddle up' was one of my mother's sayings when she hadn't a clue what she was going to do next!

If any of us arrived at the house with a load of pals unannounced, she'd 'riddle up' something to eat.

If there was some crisis of any sort and she'd 'riddle up' an answer of some sort.

So off we went for my face to be 'riddled up'.

But it wouldn't be 'riddled up' no matter what soap or cream we used, and by this time my lips were like two fat sausages, and my eyes were like 'p**s holes in the snow!'

It was approaching eleven o'clock and Hogmanay was almost here. So my mother ran to the telephone box at the end of the road, phoned the hospital and explained the situation.

They asked her if she had some paraffin stuff that was used for skin complaints in those days and she had. So she had to get cotton wool and dip it into the paraffin and wipe it gently over the sparkle. Then bring me up the next day.

So that's what we did.

I can't remember what the doctor up at the hospital said, but I remember as I went out the door with my mother to go to the hospital my father said:

'Eh dinna ken how you've got tae the age yeh hiv withoot gettin run ower beh a bus!'

Thanks, Dad!

Hogmanay Event Number Two

This happened the very next year, I think, so I guess it just shows I've a short memory, or a long learning curve!

Leading up to Hogmanay, and if you were footloose and fancy-free, you started keeping an eye out when you were at the dancing for someone to 'gae furst-fuhttin weh.' Now, this particular year my luck was in! A guy I'd taken a fancy to, asked me if I'd like to 'gae weh him' on Hogmanay.

I was over the moon! So the outfit was picked with great care, and to go with the dress (velvet I think it was) I picked a pair of three-inch, purple-coloured, sling-back high heels (Killer heels I think girls call them now, but they'll pay for it in varicose veins just like me. Oh, yes you will!) But you know what? It was worth it then (as it is now) to strut my stuff and I might have got the varicose veins in any case.

So, when it was time to set forth for the evening's entertainment, I came teetering down the stairs in my purple heels, and my mother, who'd come out to say cheerio and see me off the premises, looked at me:

'Whaur's yehr buits?'

'Eh'm no gonna bahther wearin buits this year. Eh'm jist gonna keep my new shoes on!'

'In this weather? The frost's a' ower the grund. An thir

sayin thir's mair tae come, sna' as well! So dinna be ridiculous! Go an get yehr socks an yehr buits!'

'But Ma, Eh'm no wahntin tae wear they daft buits, they dinna go weh meh frock! Naebody else's wearin buits.' *(That argument had worked successfully over a good number of years).*

'Then they're as daft as you, an Eh'm no concerned weh them!'

I said nothing. She looked at me.

'Right! Plaze yehrsel! Eh'm no gettin mehself intae a frazzle leadin up tae Hogmany ... But mind now! Eh'm tellin yeh! Dinna come greetin tae me when yehr deein o' pneumonia.'

So I didn't! Die of pneumonia that is! But I did land up *'greetin tae ehr!'*

However, the night was young and the world was my oyster as I tippy-toed off into the night on my three-inch heels to paint the town red!

Everything was fine at first because it was only frosty when we went into the Palais dance hall to meet up 'weh the rest o' them'. My Hogmanay date had turned up, so I didn't suffer the humiliation of being stood up ('duffed' in my neck of the woods)!

Then, at about eleven o'clock, I came out the dance hall to be met by ... two to three inches of snow! So I'd to slither and slide my way all through the first-footing, and by the time I got back to my house my feet were turning a bright blue!

So it was to hell with impressing my date by this time! I was home. I stuck my feet into 'meh hoosies' (slippers) quick as a whippet! Oh, the bliss of getting out of these high heels!

But the damage was done and within minutes of heating my feet up, they went from bright blue to crimson, and by now they were a-throbbing and a-thumping so fast it was like they were playing the tom-toms!

I had to see the rest of the night in, and jump about as much as possible as though I was having a good time and pray nobody leapt onto my toes,which by now felt they were going to burn right through 'meh hoosies'.

At last everybody went home and I rushed to show my mother my sore feet and seek her help!

She was finishing the tidying up as she looked at my swollen toes, but she came to my rescue as usual. Starting off with her comforting, reassuring, bedside manner:

Oh! Fir Goad's sake! Whit a mess yehr feet are in! Eh've niver seen anything like it! Well . . . Eh ken yeh dinna wahnt tae hear this, but yeh deserve it! Whit did Eh tell yeh? But then agen, thir's nae tellin you, is thir? Thir's something wrang weh you. Yehr ears jist block aff fae whit yeh dinna wahn't tae hear, an then tune in agen tae whit yeh do wahnt tae hear. Yehr jist a bliddy pest! Right let's see whit Eh'll hae tae riddle up tae deal weh this lot.

Thank you, Mother. That's made me feel so much better now!

'Whit Eh'll hae tae riddle up' was to stick my feet into a basin of hot water 'tae heat them up'. That would do the trick! Neither she nor I knew that what we were about to do was burst some of the swollen wee veins in my toes.

The agony! And now my toes looked like a bunch of wee red hot sausages!

And if my feet were throbbing before, now they could have played drums for the whole Black Watch Pipe Band!

My father must've ignored all this commotion as long as

he could, then leapt out of bed and came thundering down
the stairs:

'Dae yeh twa ken it's past three o'clock in the moarnin!
Whit the bliddy hell's a this racket?'

My mother had enough on her hands at the moment:

'Och niver mind the racket, half the street'll stull be up!
But now you're up as well, wull yeh jist *look* at the mess o'
her feet.'

He did, but by the look on his face, I think he was more
aggravated that I'd got him out of his bed!

By now I was in real agony:

'Oh! Yah! Oh! Yah Oh! Yah! OHHH! YAHHH!' *(that was me)*.

'Wull you stop that!' *(my father)*

'Whit'll weh dae now?' *(my mother)*

'Eh'll tell yeh *exactly* whit weh'll dae now! Weh'll a' go
tae wir beds, an *she'll* hae tae go tae the doctors the moarn.'
(my father)

'Meh feet are really sair *NOW!*' *(That was me again)*

'Then maybe, jist maybe, yeh should've lustened tae yehr
mither in the furst bliddy place. Well, thir's nothin that kin
be done until moarnin. An that's no sae far awa!' *(Glower
from he-whaz-no-happy-eez-night's-sleeps-been-interrupted)*. 'So
yeh'll jist *hae tae* pit up weh it then!'

And that's just what I had to do!

When I went to the doctor the next day as an emergency
appointment, I was informed I had indeed burst some of
the wee veins in my toes, and that's no picnic I can tell you.
I had to wear my most comfortable boots for weeks until
they (my toes) healed up.

When I was going the rounds of the weekend New Year
parties that carried on for weeks after Hogmanay, I had to
take my slippers with me to change into and leave the killer
heels at home!

You'll notice that risking someone dancing right onto my sore feet came second to missing out on the social whirls!

I just crippled around until I could get back into my fancy new high heels!

Ah! The joys o' bein young!

As a pensioner I seldom join in the 'Young fowk dinna listen tae anybody, they jist dae whit the like' conversations. For I'm sure that the only thing that prevented me from instant death at my father's hands when I was young, was that I only did most of the daft shenanigans to myself!

11

JANTIN IN DUNDEE

I had a jaunt ('jant' if you're a Dundonian) recently to the Continental Farmers Market that visits Dundee, and trailed round looking at all the 'stuff fae some place else'.

There was a street entertainer there with a set of drums, and he was very good. Then there was the face painting for the kids where they could come away looking like a tiger or a butterfly!

It set me to thinking about the entertainment and special events we used to have in Dundee that have more or less vanished!

When I was really wee, men used to come round the tenements and stand in the back greens and sing, tinkers would play their bagpipes, and one old man always played a melodeon, all in the hope of getting a few coppers thrown out the windows to them. This happened mostly at the weekends when they knew folk would be at home.

And then there were the rag and bone men (the raggies) who came round Fintry housing scheme with their wee vans with balloons tied onto the van. They'd stop in the street, sound their horns, or worse still (according to my father), get out the van, and blow on a trumpet, all the while yelling:

'Bring oot yehr auld claes! Bring oot yehr auld claes!' (Sounds like bring out your dead, eh?)

'Anythin at a! Anythin at a! But yeh get mair fir yehr woollens.'

Sometimes, the man would have goldfish with him, and I would try to get enough 'auld claes' to get one. Many a raggie goldfish met its demise in my house. Especially the one I 'saw off' by filling the bowl with luke-warm water one morning, after I'd come into the kitchen and discovered the water in the bowl was covered with a thin sheet of ice and felt sorry for him! Then when he started jumping all over the place I thought I'd made him happy!

It wasn't until I looked in the bowl later on and there was Goldie floating on the top of the water, dead as a dodo, that I was to learn all about the necessary requirement of oxygen to any living thing!

When I heard the raggie trumpet root-a-tootin I would fly in from wherever I was and beg my mother:

'Ma! There's the raggie! Hiv yeh got any woollens fir the raggie? Eh'll get a goldfish if yeh hiv! An if yeh've nae woollens jist gie me any auld rags! Eh need them now, afore ee goes awa!'

She would stop whatever it was she was doing:

'Eh! Eh kin hear hear him! Haud yehr horses! An eh've nae woollens the now; an Eh bet the goldfish are happy aboot that! An yehr lucky yeh dinna hae tae wear yehr auld rags like some puir sowels!'

But just the same she would go and rake and see if we had goldfish stuff! If not I had to be pleased with a balloon or a yo-yo!

* * *

When I was a kid I used to go with my mother or my granny to the Palace Theatre, which was on the site of where the Queens Hotel is now. Pantomimes were my real favourite, but later on I enjoyed acts like Lex McLean; Robert Wilson, Andy Stewart, to name a few. I used to love real old Scottish entertainment . . . until I reached my teens!

It was then I discovered the joys of, amongst other things, the Dundee ice rink. I spent many Saturday afternoons up there with my pals for a few years, whizzing round the ice.

But my real, and lasting love, was in discovering the dancing with all its jazz and rock and roll.

With the advent of the 1950s, record shops became a big deal for the younger generation, and I would sometimes spend a whole Saturday afternoon with my pals as we decided what record to buy.

If we were skint we would just pretend we were going to buy a record anyway. Then you got to go into one of the sound booths, put on the huge black earphones (or shared them if there was more than one of you), and pass the time away listening to the music, until you were asked if you were going to buy or not. Then you'd to vamoose!

Oh, and sometimes there would be some extraordinary event like a dance marathon, where you could pay to get into the dance hall and watch couples dancing until it was last man standing!

* * *

One extra special event was a guy who came to Dundee called 'Syncopating Sandy!'

Now, Sandy had set some kind of a record for playing the piano without stop for so many hours or days (I can't recall how long), and he went round the towns attempting to break this record!

So, naturally when he came to Dundee, we would have to go and see him! In my memory it was a hall somewhere up Victoria Road.

You paid two shillings to get in and in the middle of this hall 'Sandy' sat playing away on a piano. His assistants would bring his food and drink to the piano and he would feed himself as he continued to play.

But here's the thing I remember most; he had a big black curtain that they pulled across a rail that completely hid him and that was so he could change his clothes, go to the toilet . . . and all the time that piano played on! I think he was allowed some wee official breaks right enough!

The Saturday afternoon I went up to see him, I dreaded he would either need a clean shirt, or worse still, a pee! Happily none of that happened, so I just paid my money and stayed until I got fed up.

I have no idea how long it took Sandy to break his world record, or even if he did!

When I arrived home, I was relating how clever Syncopating Sandy was to all round the kitchen table as we ate our tea. When I'd finished my story, my mother said:

'That canna be guid fir that man! Ee'll be constipated weh no goin tae the lavvie fir days on end! (*How she knew Sandy hadn't 'gone tae the lavvie' was anyone's guess*). An eez fingers'll be like a pund o' sassidges! An eez bound tae be as stiff as a poker when ee's feenished a' that non-stop peeani playin!'

My father raised his hand in the 'stop' signal:

Eh dinna think Eh wahnt tae hear aboot Syncopatin Sandy's abulitions, thanks very much; especially no while Eh'm eatin!

Then he said to me:

> Did yeh say a twa shullins? Twa shullins tae stand fir
> ten meenits tae watch somebody daein a turn. An the
> place wiz choc-a-bloc! Well, Eh dinna ken aboot how
> clever ee is at playin the peeani, but eez certainly no
> *bliddy daft,* an that's fir sure!

What else could I expect from the man who'd nearly had a
tartan fit when he found out I had sent the Elvis Presley Fan
Club half a crown for a birthday record?

I was in Elvis' fan club and they sent a letter saying that
you could get a record from Elvis to celebrate one of his
birthdays with a Happy Birthday message if you sent half
a crown! Seemed like a great deal to me. The record duly
arrived with the 'special' recorded message from Elvis
himself at the beginning, followed by his latest hit 'Are You
Lonesome Tonight?' I must have driven everybody nuts by
playing that record a million times!

But for some reason known only to the god of 'How-
tae-land-yehrsel-in-hot-wahter' I told my dad where this
record came from:

> *You* sent *them* a half a croon! *You* sent *them* a half a
> croon!
> Well now Eh've heard it a'! Did yehr brehns (brains)
> go walk-aboot? Oh, eh, an anither thing! Yeh'll no need
> tae borrie (borrow) aff yehr mither this week then if
> yehr that flush!'

My mother's only comment when we were alone:

> It's yehr ain fault! Yeh should learn when tae keep yehr
> mooth shut!

So that was the end of Syncopating Sandy *and* the Elvis Fan Club!

* * *

Another venue for weekend entertainment for me was the Caird Hall Sunday Go-As-You-Pleases!

Once a month or so somebody ran a night at the Caird Hall where all the local talent could strut their stuff! A bit like the X-Factor but Dundee style!

They used to pack in the crowds and many a laugh I've had at these concerts! But do you know what? If I'd had a voice like Tina Turner you couldn't have persuaded me up on that stage! It was like taking your life in your hands!

If they loved you then that was fine: hurrahs; cheers; thunderous clapping! If they didn't then it was right to the other end of the Richter Scale with the boos, 'Get Affs', 'Gie them the Hook!'

Some of the audience even flung huppenies (halfpennies) although they were immediately ejected if they got caught!

Some of the turns were dire I have to tell you. Simon Cowell would have made mincemeat out of them! But some of them were *really* good and went on to become quite successful locally!

At the end of the evening the audience cheered the act they thought was the best and that act got the prize (whatever that was), but I tell you now, I think they should've *all* got a medal, just for having the guts!

* * *

On Sundays, you could go to the Palais in Tay Street, or the Empress Ballroom at Shore Terrace, to name two. Although you couldn't have a dance, you could sit and have a cup of coffee or a soft drink and eye up the talent, or just walk round meeting up with folk and having a blether.

If you preferred walking outside then there was always the Sunday Monkey Parade, where you could just wander up and down the old Overgate to your heart's content!

There were clubs open on Sunday like the Parker Street Jazz Club and the Continental Ballroom, so if I'd any money to spare I sometimes went there!

Can you imagine now, a time when the pictures, the pubs, the dancing and the shops were all closed on Sunday?

* * *

I remember when television heralded the end for many picture houses in Dundee.

Later on we were introduced to a new form of entertainment; the Bingo! Greens Playhouse was amongst the first of the cinemas to re-open as a bingo hall.

I remember my mother and I giving the Greens bingo a 'go' after it opened, and that was us hooked on our weekly 'Housie-Housie' afternoon out! We spent lots of our Saturday afternoons there, for years.

Back then (the 1970s and 1980s) they just left the cinema as it was, so you had to get yourself a special 'bingo board' to clip your bingo tickets onto as you had no table. A vast difference from todays bingo halls!!

* * *

Nowadays, we have an entertainment that was far beyond our ken when I was a youngster! It's called computers that link to the Internet!

You can inhabit a cyberspace world that we would have thought of as science fiction when I was a kid! And just as I loved all the sci-fi movies with the silver cardboard spaceships, I love the Internet!

I know it absolutely has its down points and can be a

dangerous place, but as an information and shopping tool I think it is grand! As for computers, I would've been old and wizened (no comments from my nearest and dearest, please) before this book was finished, if I'd had to write it in long hand!

My mother would have given her eye teeth to just sit at a computer (as I do) and trawl round this huge supermarket via the Internet (no running round all the shops as your bags pile up, and then having to humph them all the way home on the bus).

Then a couple of days later a man knocks on my door and brings in all the bags and I haven't even had to leave the house to do any of the hard work!

I can just hear her:

Daen yehr shoppin without lahvin the hoose, wid yeh believe it? An money jist taen oot yehr bank account! Well, there yeh go! Haein a bankie book in the furst place! An buyin a month's messages a in one go . . . Happy Days!

But isn't it grand that yeh *hiv* the money tae dae a yehr shoppin at once, as lang as they didna treh an palm aff a' thir auld stuff on yeh (*rest assured, Mother, they don't*). Well, anything that maks yehr life easier gets meh vote!

And she would mean it!

* * *

So Dundee, like the rest of the world, moves forward into an ever-changing new world of technology.

Speaking to someone at the other end of the world via a computer, how cool is that! Long ago when one of your family went away to far-off lands, you could bet it was only a photograph that would let you see them from then on!

TVs the size of small cinema screens in your own home, on line shopping, phones you can plug in your ear (a far cry from the telephone box at the end of the road), and many other 'things' that would have just been a dream when I was a kid!

So, what will the entertainment of the future be I wonder? Plugs you just stick in your ears and off you go to have a part in the film you're about to watch? And it can't be that far away when you will select a place you want to go on holiday from the Internet, step into the tube they'll have in the shops and hey presto, Dundee to Mars in twenty nanoseconds! Dan Dare eat your heart out!

* * *

However, one thing I hope they don't ever change is one very important part of our world . . . us!

My mother used to say; 'The mair things cheenge, the mair they bide the same!'

That thought crossed my mind as I sat on the bus, going into town, one cold winter's day not long ago.

The stop after I got on the bus two young lassies got on and not a coat between them! One of them had a short-sleeved shirt and the other one just had on a cardigan, and they both had on the wee skirts and leggings that they wear nowadays. They were also talking to each other while they spoke to someone else on their mobiles!

I gave a mental shiver as they walked past me and I thought:

Geezo if they twa dinna hae pneumonia afore they get hame, Eh'm a monkey's uncle! An they mobiles are niver oot o' they young anes ears. Thi'll be dafe afore thir thirty!

Hard on its heels another thought thundered in:

Oh! Meh Goad! It's happened! Eh've morphed intae meh mither an father!

That was quickly followed by:

Eh must be getting auld right enough! Och well! Whit kin yeh dae?

As I sat there, lost in my thoughts, and envying (in a small way) the two skimpily dressed kids at the back of the bus, who were still yattering away to each other, *and* someone else in cyberspace, a smile crossed my lips as, for no reason at all, I recalled something else my mother said to me one day, after she'd paid a visit to the doctor:

Geezo! Eh must be gettin auld. Thir wiz a lassie in the doctor's weh a bairn in a Tansad, an she looked like she should've been in a Tansad ehrsel! Even the doctor looked like ee should've been at the skale, instead o' in a doctor's surgery helpin tae soart me oot!

Another thunderbolt just landed!
Now, I know *exactly* what she meant!
Then, I swear I heard a wee wummin's voice, sounding remarkably like my mother, whispering in my ear:

Telt yeh!

12

GOIN TAE THE PICTURES

I have always loved 'goin tae the pictures', and I think going to the cinema is one of the finest forms of escapism there is.

However, with all the new style televisions, 'goin tae the pictures' has arrived right to your own fireside! If it's a choice of a film on the television, or almost anything else, then you'll find me, feet up on the pouffe, ready to travel away into whatever world will be extended to me for a couple of hours. Better still if it's on in the evening, then it's into the 'jammies' first, then feet up on the pouffe and I'm off with Brad Pitt to help him kill off all the Trojans! And yes I do know that the Trojans were the goodies, but when it's them or Brad Pitt, then whose side I'm on is 'no contest!'

From the day my older brother took me by the hand and led me through the door of the Princess Cinema Club up the Hawkhill, where the University grounds are today, until now, when the big screens with all their graphics and computerisation can really take you into the fantasy world of your choice, escaping into an adventure beyond the world I live in has always appealed to me!

However, when I was a kid and went to the cinema club,

I can't say I liked when it was my turn to 'sneaky in'. We did this if my brother's two pals were there and then we split the extra money. If it was my turn for the sneaky-in, then I'd join the queue to get into the cinema club, having waved goodbye to my mother with her promising;

'See yeh *right here* when the pictures come oot. Behave now!'

Then we four would join the pushing and shoving that went on at the big two-door entrance to the cinema club that was literally just two steps up from the pavement, and then inside to the wee box-office window where the girl took your money and issued the tickets.

Now, here's the bit I didn't like. I'd to drop down on all fours and crawl beneath the other threes' legs, then creep along as they each put their money up and said:

'Sixpenny seat, please.'

It wasn't the first time when I was crawling along that I could see a bum in front of me, so I guess it must have been their 'sneaky-in' turn as well.

So hurdle one over, I could stand up and get my share of the prize money.

Hurdle two was down at the end of the corridor in the form of the 'The Chief Usher' (or in our case 'Public Enemy Number One') who took the tickets, checked to see the date on them and then did a head count.

So we'd wait until the crowd were all dashing through the entrance to the seating area and just run at the man, throw our tickets into his hands and fly past him in the hope he wouldn't be able to see us in the mob!

And you know what? Most of the time we got away with it! If he did catch us, then he *kept* the three tickets that had been paid for and the four of us got thrown out, so we couldn't just pay the extra ticket. But my brother used to like the danger, I think, and just said when we got frog-marched into the street:

'Well, weh'll jist hae tae play aboot here so that Ma dizna ken weh've got the boot fae the pictures 'cause weh did a sneaky-in!'

We might have been young and foolish, but brain dead we weren't, so we just used to spend what little money we had left at the shop across from the cinema, then later on run back down the lane at the side of the cinema where the exits were and join the hoards as they ran up the road after the show, where we would meet up with our real life chief.

If we got past the first minute without:

Dinna gie me that Hiya Ma, the pictures wir great the day. Mrs So-and-So (*Canna-keep-ehr-mooth-shut' as far as we were concerned*) seen the twa o' yeh playin aboot the street, while the pictures were in, an met me jist twa meenits ago, an telt me as Eh wiz comin up the road. Whit hiv yeh done?

Then we were home and dry, and just blethered a load of rubbish about the films that were shown because we knew she only half listened to us anyway! You had to be able to live on the edge if you hung about with my older brother, but one thing was for sure, life with him was *never* dull!

Dundee had many picture houses. I think at one time there were over thirty, so as I grew to be a teenager, they were just an extension of the cinema club that I used to go to as a kid.

Going to the pictures was one of our main forms of entertainment. They used to change the programmes twice a week, and for your money you got the Pathe News introduced by a cockerel (don't ask me why), the trailers for what was coming up next, a wee picture, and then the BIG picture.

There were usually two showings at the weekends and you could just come and go as you pleased. If you were at the last showing it was head for the door as soon as they put up 'The End' because they played the national anthem after that!

I absolutely love horror movies!

When I was old enough to see X-rated movies, I used to go with my pals to the Cinerama in Tay Street where they specialised in horror films such as *Dracula bites again!* or *Creature from the Black Lagoon*, where the mummy waded through every swamp in America trailing his bandages behind him.

Oh, here's a thing about that mummy. He could only go at a crawl because of his wet muddy bandages and that limp he always had, but no matter how fast the folk he was chasing ran away (or even *drove* away), they would stop running/driving, draw breath to indicate they were safe (hoping to lull you into a false security, but you knew better), then who would just up and appear at the end of the road that was a hundred miles away from the original spot . . . but that mummy. He was some guy! Wet bandages or not!

And what's up with that heroine who searches the swamps (with not a hair out of place) in the dead of night to try to save her boyfriend from the mummy? Yeh, right! As if any sane person would do that! If you'd the sense you were born with, and after you'd stopped your hair from standing on end, you'd hot-foot it out of there and let him take his chances with the mummy. It's his own fault for going near a swamp in the first place!

One of my particular favourites was *Dracula*. Any *Dracula* would do, but I loved Bella Lugosi the best; he used to make me watch the picture through the buttonhole in my coat!

There was one particular film showing on this night we were at the pictures, where the heroine was getting strangled to death as old Draccie-boy sucked her blood from her porcelain white throat. And one of these guys sitting behind us, who had been pestering us, grabbed one of my pals by the throat saying in a deep throaty Dracula voice, 'Die! . . . Die! . . . Die . . .' just like Bella.

Well, we all about laid an egg and let out screams that reverberated right out the picture house and up to the Law Hill, after which, we were all promptly evicted by the usher and usherette who were on duty, much to the relief of the rest of the patrons of the Cinerama I would imagine, and before the woman who'd been tut-tutting louder than the bats were shrieking had sent her husband to get us 'punted-oot' anyway.

At least I didn't have to run up and down Tay Street until the pictures came out so that I could fool my mother, so that was a bonus.

* * *

There was this one other time I got thrown out the pictures when I was older.

I was sitting in the front row of the balcony (must've robbed a bank that day), of what used to be the King's Theatre, that was across the road from the Wellgate.

The place was choc-a-bloc, but the seats in the balcony shaped round in an arc, so of course the corner seats at the wall had the least leg room and the worst view, and were to be dodged at all costs.

So when the picture house filled up the usherette would flash her torch and request that we all, 'Move along, please!'

to which the patron who would be landing up at the wall seats would reply:

'Eh didna come in early tae land at the wa. Thi'll jist hae tae squeeze past.'

So that's what the latecomers had to do. *Say*, 'Excuse me. Eh'm really sorry,' to every set of toes they stood on, as they made their way to the wall seats.

And it was that situation that caused all the bother that night I got 'threw oot'!

I'd bought a big Eldorado ice cream to eat during the film (definitely must've come into money), and went early so that I could get my coat and all my other 'stuff' on the floor and the ledge of the balcony, as there was plenty space if you were in the start of the first row.

So the lights are down, the trailers are on, when down comes one of the ushers with this pair of latecomers, who must have decided they would take the two scabby seats at the wall.

The usherette flashes her torch along our row.

'Excuse me, could you let these people in?'

I guess she had decided a move-along rammy was not a good idea as the big picture was about to begin.

So, like everybody else, I was muttering away about 'Bliddy pests'. So that I could pick up my coat and other junk I had with me, I put my opened Eldorado ice cream with the wee spoon stuck in it on the ledge of the balcony, as I didn't want ice cream all over my coat.

And yes you've got it!

As the guy pushed past me he shoved the Eldorado over the balcony, and all you heard in the dark was 'AAAAAAAAAH-HHHHH!' as my ice cream hit one of the punters sitting in the stalls down below, right on the head and all over him (from what I heard later).

So, if there was a 'stushie' about getting to the seats in the front row of the balcony before, there was now a real 'stushie' from the guy who's covered in ice cream, who's now going to wreak all kinds of vengeance on the 'Eedjit wha did that!'

The upshot was we (the rest of them who were with me got the turf as well) all got thrown out the pictures.

I had no intention of going quietly this time! To hell with all the requests to 'SHHHUUUSSHHTT!' and 'Oh, fir Goad's sake. Whit a racket,' and so forth!

I hadn't been the one to start all the rumpus (in my opinion):

> It wiz they twa at the wa's fault. They should hae been at the pictures in time, and no hid abody else jumpin up an doon! An how are they no gettin threw oot as well?

By this time, we were in the main aisle at the top of the stairs and the whole picture house was a-shushing! And I was a-shushing right back!

The usherette decided she'd be better off working in Woolies round the corner and had called the manager, who in turn said that I should never have put my ice cream on the ledge of the balcony. I gave him the 'Whit-aboot-they-ither-ains' rant, and he gave us free passes for another time, just to shut us up. Then he turfed us all out anyway!

With the passage of time, my pals and I graduated to going to the pictures with a 'date', which back in my time meant only two of you. My feelings when I see three teen-agers sitting together in cinemas nowadays, where one of them might be a couple and one a pal, is good for them!

Back when I was their age it would've been unthinkable to go out with your pal when she had a date, or was 'goin steady'.

* * *

There used to be two prices for the pictures and, if it was a popular picture and very busy, then they would put a sign outside on the pavement saying 'Balcony queue here' or 'Stalls queue here' and you went into the queue that you could afford!

I don't know too much about the rituals nowadays, but back then it was also unheard of to offer to pay your own way when some guy had first asked you out! If I didn't go into the 'Balcony' queue on a *first* date, that lad never got rated much.

When I think about it, too bad if the poor guy was skint! And if he'd asked me to pay my own way, then that was definitely the end of him! But the one thing that was the girls' job when you were off to a night at the pictures with some lad was to bring the sweeties.

Usually, the first place everybody went with a lad who had asked you out was the Greens Playhouse which was very up-market as far as we were all concerned.

The Greens Playhouse had a huge café at the front of house where you could have a soft drink or tea/coffee if you were early for the picture. The tea/coffe was served in china cups and saucers, and they had special wee silver teaspoons usually reserved for toffs! It had leather settees and, if memory serves me, art deco wallpaper and lights.

The staircases and the vast foyer had marble pillars and floors. Inside the auditorium (easy seen I'm not at the Princess Cinema Club now) was the biggest stage, and the longest fanciest velvet curtains that were operated by electric switches and swished open as the news came on.

Upstairs in the balcony there were theatre-type boxes along the sides of the walls that were separated by more velvet curtains, and there were runner carpets down all the aisles and even into the rows where the seats were. Having carpets all over a cinema wasn't the norm in those days and lots of cinemas only had runners down the front of house and down the aisles. Then you were on to the boards.

Oh, and the ladies room in the Greens had about twenty toilets and a separate place with some mirrors for titivating yourself! Actually it really *was* beautiful inside!

My father (an electrician) worked on the Greens when it was being built. I remember him telling us about when they were working on the sign outside which spelt 'Greens Playhouse' in a huge neon vertical line with the 'U' slanted out from the rest of the letters, that they wanted the 'U' that way; to represent 'We want you in.' Clever, eh?

Upstairs were the dear seats. The front four rows of the balcony were the dearest along with the boxes down the side. Then the further back you went in the balcony, it got a little cheaper! There was also another wee café just at the bottom of the stairs that you walked up to gain access to the balcony.

The boxes (ashtrays) housed small two-people settees and were officially called 'Golden Divans'; known locally as the 'Golden Dehve-Ons'.

These 'chummy seats' were a place that I would never ever go on a first date, because that might be seen as a 'green light' (a green light in the Greens that could be a song) to your date that he could 'treh-yeh-on' (work that one out for yourselves). So the front row of the balcony it was, and that's exactly what I answered, in double time, to the usherette who took the tickets, after we'd climbed the staircase that led on to the balcony.

She'd flash her torch down onto the ticket and then ask;

'Golden Divans or Front rows?'

'Front Rows Please.' *(No way was I giving a first date any ideas)*.

The ushers/usherettes used to patrol the 'Golden Dehve-Ons' during the evening, flashing away with their torches just to make sure there was no real hanky-panky going on.

One of my mother's friends was an usherette there for a spell, and when I was older she used to have us in stitches about some of the things she'd seen when she was on 'torch duty.'

Can you picture being in the throes of passion and some buggar shining a light on you and saying;

'Hey whit's goin on here?' *(As if they couldn't see)*. 'That's enough o' that if yeh don't mind!'

Well, even if you *did* mind, it would be enough right enough, when you were under the spotlight and all and sundry were now trying to eyeball through the dark to look in your direction and see if they knew you!

I leave all of you who can remember those times, (or decided to forget them as the case may be) with your own memories of the Greens Playhouse and the Golden 'Dehve-Ons'.

* * *

That last paragraph has made me think that the one thing that has changed drastically is the topics that can be shown on the big screen.

When I was young if the Indian scalped a white man it was absolutely bloodless. When James Cagney jumped from the roof of that oil tank shouting 'It's me, Ma!' there wasn't even a dint in the pavement.

I watched a picture the other night on television where the baddie ate everybody he could lay hands one, cut out a guy's brains' fried them and fed them back to the guy . . . and that was only for starters (pardon the pun). Then he ripped folks' faces off right, left and centre. I was almost forced to watch it through the button hole of my housecoat!

The old film baddies like Bella Lugosi (Dracula) and his vampire bat that dangled on the end of a string, which was as clear as daylight for all to see, would've run a mile the minute that guy got his 'Gie-me-yehr-boady-tae-eat' knife out!

But, just like back then, I have always enjoyed being half scared to death when watching a film, so I watched that television picture from beginning to end and then put on all the lights and tried the door to make sure it was locked before I went to bed. No way was I going to be supper for 'Auld Chomp-yehr-face-aff-as-quick-as-Eh-look-at-yeh!'

Shades of my older brother running ahead of me when we came out the cinema up the West End then he would pounce out one of the closes, hands in the air, yelling:

The Beassssst weh fehve finnnngers, (a hand with no body that prowled around somewhere in America murdering folk who wandered in deserted places in the dead of night – the numpties); helped beh DRAAACULLAAAA . . . are cominnnnn tae get yeeeehhhhh . . . an drink yehr blood . . . an choke yeeehhhh tae deeaaathhthth.

I would duly scream my head off at him;
'If you dae that agen Eh'm really gonna tell Dad on yeh, an then yeh'll be fir it in earnest fir no lookin efter me right!

But he'd just toss his imaginary crimson and black cloak over his shoulder, wipe the imaginary blood from his mouth and vanish into the night to look for his next close!

* * *

Anyway back to the cinema and the one thing that has changed beyond any recognition is sex in Cinemas! No . . . not *actual sex* in cinemas. I think you'd still get the bounce nowadays if they caught you doing that, but Sex on the cinema screen!

If there was a bedroom scene in the films long ago, then the heroine had to be in the bed practically fully clothed, or with enough frills round her body to make a pair of net curtains for a ten-foot bay window. The hero had to be leaning over her, but not touching. When they kissed it was like two canaries pecking, and the rules were that he kept one foot on the floor at all times. He never even got his *jumper* off (never mind his whole kit) before it faded to black.

When I was in my thirties, I remember going with my mother to see that picture about the wee dwarf that's meant to be a ghost, running around Venice in her red raincoat slitting everyone's throat, when to my horror, halfway through the picture, this really explicit bedroom scene started taking place between the hero and the heroine, with my mother sitting right at my elbow.

It was one of these moments when you think; 'Well that's the best buht actin Eh've seen in meh puff,' and there was one of these hushes fell over the place apart from a titter here and there.

When into this silence my mother nudges me, and says in the loudest whisper I have ever heard:

'In the name o' Goad! Whit's goin on here? Are they actin

or whit? Hiv they twa nae dignity, makin a show o' thirsels like that? Now Eh've seen it a' an no mistake!'

Well, she got that right I can tell you! There were no quiet sniggers then. The whole place round about us erupted, as my mother just carried on munching her sweeties.

If I'd had a hat with me I would've stuck it over my face.

Nowadays it's totally different, nudity is not an issue. And you know what? So what! When I speak about then and now, I am careful not to fall into the 'passing judgement' trap! I just say it's a lot different! And it is!

* * *

It's just dawned on me that I never once mentioned in this chapter that I like *Cinderella* and *Sleeping Beauty*, and films that are 'whistle-while-you-workie' as well.

But for me it will always be a blood and thunder and adventure. Or, the film that makes you jump out of your shirt when you least expect it, and better still you're just recovering from a previous jump-out-your-shirt moment when up leaps another heart stopper!

I was at the cinema recently to see one of the Harry Potter films! It was magnificent! The graphics, the stunts, and the illusions, were all very clever and second to none. I sat there with my goodies, in the fancy seat with its can/bottle holder, the seat with its high back where you could rest your head, and you're all on a tiered level so that you can see without somebody's 'big heid' blocking your view, Quadra-sound in operation (or whatever it's called), that would make your tinnitus do the Highland Fling, and there I was, ducking the flying hockey players as they flashed overhead. *Magic!*

And there's loads of other things in multiplex cinemas nowadays: games; hot and cold food; seating areas; loads of toilets. Oh, and toilet roll holders with two toilet rolls in them and one on the cistern for spare. Then a note telling you when the toilets were last inspected and asking, if you're not happy, to let them know!

The only fault is that with all these new technologies a visit to the cinema is not cheap anymore!

A far cry from the Saturday Cinema Club where there was linoleum on the floors, trying to listen in vain to what the actors on the screen were saying above the noise of all the real-life actors, prompters, cheerers and booers, that were watching the picture. No screen the size of the High Street. Wooden seats that clattered like giant building blocks, and that had a big space between the seat and the back rest, so that you were always in a fight with the person behind you, who thought it was alright to stick their shoes up into the space at the back of your seat and rest them on your bum! No foyer to speak about!

One or two wee toilets that constantly ran out of toilet paper, and you were meant to tell one of the ushers if you used the last of it so that they could replace it, but you didn't care because it wasn't going to be you that would have to do without (at least not that time). One wee sink with cold water that you never bothered to wash your hands in anyway, and if you did then you just wiped them on your clothes as you dashed back into the hall! Good picture time was a wasting!

As for letting the staff of the cinema know that someone had peed on the floor or such like, well we just dodged around it and ignored it!

But you know what! No matter the comfort or sanitary differences that have spanned almost sixty-five years of cinema going in my case, the feeling of escapism and excitement as I was carried along with that Harry Potter adventure was exactly the same as it was nearly sixty-five years ago when I first fell in love with the Lone Ranger, Zorro, and all the rest of them!

Some things in our lives never change right enough ... thank goodness! For me 'goin tae the pictures' has always been one of them.

* * *

I wonder what cinemas will be providing in the way of entertainment when I'm ninety?

I bet you'll just go into a big hall (well, I hope there will still be cinemas to have a night out to), there'll be no screen or anything like that. You'll just plug yourself into a computerised seat, select a film, and away you'll go. There might even be a way you can imagine that you're one of the actors in the picture and living the adventure instead of just watching it! And, of course, there will be a facility for a few of you to plug in and act in the same film!

Shove over Brad!

I can't wait!

13

DANCIN AT THE PALAIS AN THE LAST TRAM HAME

Dancing was a huge part of my life from the time I was fourteen up until I was twenty, and I guess that would be the same for at least ninety-five per cent of young Dundonians back in the 1950s, who were in my age group.

Dundee had quite a few dance halls in these days.

The love of my dancing memories will always be 'Roabies' because it was my first 'grown-up' entertainment. Robertson's dance hall was up the West End of the City where I was brought up as a kid, and when I was older, and got permission, I jived the night away there at least three times a week, until it was approaching the 1950s, and I graduated from 'Roabies' to the dancing in general.

I completely skipped the 'normal' dance halls where lots of youngsters, who didn't dedicate themselves to becoming the best jiver that they could be, attended. They went to places like Kidds Rooms, which was somewhere near the City Churches if I recall correctly.

I remember one of my pals telling me that Kidds had 'school corners' where various members who'd gone to the same school hung out. However, it wasn't like that picture *West Side Story*, where they were at daggers drawn, and just went about murdering each other. I think it was much more genteel than that!

Then, there was the JM Ballroom at the bottom of the West Port, The Parker Street Jazz Club, The Continental Ballroom next to the SCWS at the bottom of the Wellgate, the Empress dance hall across from Shore Terrace, where you could hear all the great bands of that era such as Sid Phillips and his orchestra live, and it was a full orchestra, and the Clyde Valley Stompers (my very own favourite).

Oh, and we used to go on the bus up to a place called the Reid Halls in Forfar. Or down to a dance hall called The Chalet that was at Broughty Ferry, just beside the water.

But my graduation from Roabies was to the Palais De' Dance (the Palais) in Tay Street.

When I was seventeen, I decided that my 'Roabies 'uniform had to go. I entered a more grown-up stage where I just wore my own type of clothing, but I still had a strict dress code! If my older sister or my mother said:

'Eh Really like that blouse/skirt (whatever) yeh've on. Yeh really suit it.' Then 'it' immediately got the boot.

I can remember when my father would throw a doubt on some of my attire, my mother would just say:

'Och she might as well be deid as oot the fashion.'

To which he would invariably reply:

'Well, beh the sight o' that she's well alehve an kickin.'

But then he knew as much about fashion as a tee totaller in a brewery.

However, the line was drawn when I pranced down the stairs in my very first mini skirt and he caught sight of me before I could escape out the door:

'Hold it right there! Whit the hell's that yeh've *no* got on.'

'Meh new skirt. Abody's wearin them.'

'Eh couldna care less if the world an eez wife's wearin

them. Yeh're no goin oot weh that pelmet on. Now jist get back up they stairs an pit on somethin half decent.'

So I did. I guess that was one of the big differences between my father and my mother. With my mother, the 'debate' took at least half an hour, even if I lost in the end. With my father, the debate took zero minutes when he made up his mind!

So, I just put a longer skirt on over the top of my mini skirt, put in an appearance, and then just hopped out the door, with a departing glower from 'He-wha-izna-happy', and went on my merry way. I bet there are more than a few out there who recall that caper. But it kept my father happy, and that was the wise thing to do!

One fashion that came in when I went to the Palais was the huge puffy-out skirts with all the underskirts beneath them that created a 'fairy-aff-the-tap-o-the-tree' look, and that made you think you were Doris Day. Or if the skirt was floppy, then you got an underskirt that you could slide a huge plastic hoop through the hem of, and that made your skirt stick out even further. The only thing was when you sat down on the seats at the side of the hall, you had to be really careful, or everybody could see what you had for your breakfast if your skirt wheeched up at the front.

The Palais in Tay Street was the most popular dance hall in Dundee, and the queue to get in on Friday or Saturday reached down the long entrance into the dance hall and right into Tay Street.

They had bouncers on the doors back then as well. If they thought some guy was drunk, he didn't even get into the hall, and there were no bars inside dance halls in these days.

They also had bouncers that patrolled the dance floor to ensure that trouble of any kind was dealt with as soon as possible; dance hall 'watchies' in a way. These attendants wore white gloves. I suppose it was just to distinguish them from the guys on the door, because they certainly didn't look like they'd just done the dishes!

Back in my days the 'drinking thing' was all a bit one-sided though. Nearly all the pubs were men-only in the bar. The norm was for the girls to get into the dancing at about 9 p.m., but the guys went to the pub, and came in at about 10 p.m.-ish when most of the pubs shut. So, since we didn't want to dance with each other for an hour, we used to do a lot of our 'dancing dollying up' in the ladies cloakroom before the hall filled up.

Once we were a bit older we did, of course, sneak into the wee ladies' lounges in the pubs. These areas were called 'snugs', and were a room off the main bar. There we would order a Babycham (kiddie-on champagne that was affordable) before we went into the dancing. And if we had more than two Babychams we thought we were real ravers. But . . . if anybody who knew your folks came into that pub, you practically glued yourself to the wall of the snug in case you'd been spotted.

The ladies' cloakroom in the Palais was downstairs. It had seats in front of the mirrors where you could freshen up your make-up. It had a perfume machine on the wall where you could get a scoosh of perfume for sixpence, I think it was, and the perfumes had exotic names like 'Midnight in Paris' or 'Ashes of Roses'; just the job for a place called the Palais De'Dance.

In those days, we didn't have enough money to have a wardrobe full of clothes, and my pals and I used to go into the toilet and swap clothes if we were fed up with what we'd on.

I used to wear my cardigan back to front so that it doubled up as a jumper, and I would stick a plastic collar round the neckline, which scratched my neck all night, but looked good.

Oh, and what about this? Only guys with black top coats were 'in' as far as I was concerned. Guys who wore white raincoats were a no-no. How you told a black raincoat guy from a white raincoat guy when you were up dancing with him was anybody's business.

If I'd met someone I'd fancied that night and he asked me 'hame', the place to meet my 'click' was always at 'the-tap-o-the-stairs' near the door, and at going home time the foyer was packed with guys waiting for who they were 'gaen up the road weh.'

When I got to the top of the stairs, I would look around nonchalantly, until I spied my date. It was in that short space of time that I always wondered what I'd do if he'd changed his mind and I was left high and dry. I don't remember it ever happening to me, but I wouldn't put it in a book that I'd been stood-up ('duffed') anyway! If the guy I'd pulled that night had on a white raincoat well that was just too bad on me!

Oh, and another taboo! I would *never* meet any of my dates under the clock at Samuel's corner at the bottom of Reform Street. That was because it was famous for being called 'Duffers' Corner'. If the person you were waiting for never turned up then you looked like a real lemon as the whole of Dundee passed by with a 'yeh've been duffed' wee smile at your expense!

Also if you got duffed, you immediately told all your pals, and in Dundee parlance as far as I was concerned: 'That wiz his erse oot the windie'. He just got ignored from then on in. Duffing someone was only excusable as far as I was concerned if you were on crutches the next time I saw you.

Inside the dance halls, if you'd refused some lad who'd

asked you to dance, then you were meant to sit that dance out, and if you went up with someone you fancied better, and the guy you'd just refused took it into his head to point you out to one of the white-gloved brigade, then the bouncer would cross the dance floor and stop you in the middle of the dance and give you trouble. So if I did go up and dance with someone else after I'd refused, then I just kept my fingers crossed, and tried to hide by dancing as much as possible in the middle of the hall!

The one dance I didn't like was 'Ladies' Choice'. It was then I appreciated what the guys had to go through if they crossed the floor and got a knock-back from whomever they asked up to dance. So he had to be a real pest or 'no-hoper' before I ever refused a dance to anyone. And I just used to sit Ladies' Choice out unless I knew the guy I was asking up!

You weren't allowed to dance too close at the slow dances. And if you did, then the bouncer would appear once again, tap the guy on the shoulder and just wave his hands in a 'move back a wee buhttie' gesture, then walk away.

So, even in the dancing, you had to behave to a set of rules, just like at the cinema club when I was a kid, but at least in the cinema club when the lights went down you got to leap about any way you wanted. But I wasn't at the cinema club any more. Life in general, and the new rules in particular, were a lot more complicated.

On special nights in the Palais they used to string nets with balloons in them across the middle of the roof, then during a dance, and without any warning, the balloons would come cascading down.

Now, this balloon cascade wasn't just to give you some extra fun. The management used to put tickets in the balloons that gave you a free night at the dancing the following week. Talk about man mind thyself! It was a real free for all with folk jumping all over the place bursting balloons, just to see if there was a free ticket in them.

I did join in the 'balloon thing' if I was there, but I much preferred ironing my older brother's shirts and getting dancing money from him. Much safer when you're five feet nothing in your stocking soles I can tell you!

A huge sparkly ball hung from the ceiling in the Palais and used to spin round during the slow dances, when the lights were dimmed. At the last dance, this ball would spray wee sparkly lights out all over the hall. The last tune of the evening was always 'Who's Taking You Home Tonight?' Fine and dandy if you'd just clicked with someone you'd been eyeing for ages, but tough luck on you if the answer to 'Who's Taking you Home Tonight?' was 'Naebody cause Eh've no got a click the night!'

When I did let a guy see me 'Up the road fae the dancin', if it was a first date then you just stood at the front gate with him. After a few dates then we got to stand at the front door. But about fifteen minutes after we got to the gate or the door, I would hear the rattle of milk bottles from inside the house. If I didn't make a move to say cheerio, then a few minutes later there would be a cough and a rattle of the milk bottles. I made a move then alright, because the time I defied all this 'father-Morse-code business', my father just opened the door and said:

'Hi there, son. You . . . come in *(points at me)*. You . . . go hame' *(points at him)*.

Then he ushered me in and shut the door on whoever it was with a 'Cheerio then' to the back of the guy who's now thinking what a narrow escape he's had. He might've asked me out again, and had to come *inside* the house!

Had he but known my father tried with all his might

to just ignore most of who gathered round the kitchen table (apart from my real pals) that were with me, and usually just gave a nod and hello as he walked through the room!

We never ever would have thought of getting a taxi home after the dancing, no matter how late it got out. The dancing closed in time for folk to get the last bus. And there used to be a couple of late buses, and then it was Shanks pony.

About one of the first questions a guy who was interested in you asked was where you lived. When I asked my older brother what this was all about, he told me this was because if the lad asked you home and you lived miles away, then after he'd seen you home he'd to hoof it back to where he stayed.

Sometimes, your date only walked you to the bus station at Shore Terrace, so that he could get a bus home as well. So he'd to fancy you right enough the first time he asked you up the road if you lived at the other end of the town from him! But at least it proved he was keen on you!

There were a couple of late trams that ran after the buses went off and they stopped at the terminus at Maryfield, so, it was nothing for loads of youngsters to come off the last tram on Friday/Saturday night, and walk all the way home to Fintry.

My older sister told me that if she and her pal missed the last bus home, they used to sometimes practise their dance steps with some of the guys they knew who lived near us, after they got off the bus at the Maryfield terminus, and before they started the trek home to Fintry,

Now it was one of the last buses home that caused a whole lot of bother in my house one Friday night.

* * *

My older sister was now going steady with her future husband. He must have been visiting for his tea, and now it was time for him to leave to get the last bus home and she was going with him to walk him to the bus stop.

Unknown to any of us in the house, when they'd got to the end of our street, they were met by my older brother coming home, who informed them he'd just come *off* the last bus and that it was away, so my sister's lad would have to walk up to Maryfield to get the last tram home instead. Then my brother and sister decided that they would walk with him up to Maryfield to keep him company, then she would have my brother to walk home with, so that was alright.

Good plan, apart from the fact that they'd both lived with my mother all their lives up to now, and decided to just not appear without letting anyone know.

* * *

When we were all old enough to be going out and about ourselves, no matter what time we came in, you just got your key in the lock when her voice shouted down the stairs: 'Wha's that?'

That's when we went into our 'Me-Ma' identification mode. This went on until we were all home, and she could finally get to sleep.

So, half an hour after my sister had left home, my mother says to my father:

'Whaur the hell is she? The bus stop's only twa meenits awa, an the last bus is lang gone.'

'She's possibly met somebody an thir hain a blether at the end o' the street or somethin like that.' *(my father)*

'Well, Eh'm goin oot tae hae a look.'

And off she trots to look up the street. The door opens then closes again.

'Thir's nae sign o' ehr. No even in the street.'

'Gie it anither fehve meenits.' *(my father)*

'Na! Eh'm no happy! So, you get yehr coat on *(that was to me)*, an you kin wait here on us comin back, in case she comes hame anither road *(that was to my father)* weh'll possibly meet ehr half wey alang the street!'

So we set off on sister-hunt with my mother chuntering on:

'Honest tae Goad! Whit is she thinkin o'? She kens Eh'd be worried seek if she took too lang. If it hid been you that'd gone missin Eh'd hae kent it wiz some daft caper that hid held *you* up *(thanks, Mother)*, but she wid niver gie me a worry like this!

'An whaur's the bold boy? *(my older brother)* He should've been up the road ana, but it's no sae bad fir him Eh dinna suppose!'

No, maybe not, I thought? He maybe *knew* the axe murderer, so that should keep him safe!

By this time, we had reached the end of our street without meeting another soul. We approached the open ground where new houses were being built.

'Right,' says she, pulling out a torch (yes she had brought a torch with her), 'let's start lookin in they foonds (foundations). She could've slipped an knocked erhsel unconscious an be lehin conked oot doon some o them!'

We must've looked like Burke and Hare as we trawled around the wasteground in the pitch black with the torch. Where was a Watchie when you needed them?

Hallelujah! Nothing down the foundations! Thank goodness! I've never been good with real life blood!

'Right that's it! Eh'm aff up tae the Boabies box! C'mon!'

So saying, she dragged me at a half run for the next couple of streets, until we came to the local police box, where she about battered the door down.

'Hello there. Is anybody in? Are yeh in?'

The wee square peep hole flew open.

'Meh Goad, whit's up, missus?

'Eh've lost meh lassie. She's gone missin. She never diz anythin like this! Eh'm worried seek!'

'Calm yersel. Right come in oot the cauld. How lang hiz she been gone?

'Jist aboot over an oor, maybe even a wee bit mair.'

'Now! Gie me ehr description.'

'She aboot meh sehze, but she's got blonde hair, an blue eyes. An Eh think she'd on a green coat and suede buits.'

'Age?'

'Twenty-two.'

The policeman stopped writing and looked up from his notepad. First at her, then at me, then at her again!

'*Twenty-two?*'

'Eh, an . . .'

'Missus, Eh canna report a wummin o' twenty-two missin, jist efter an oor or so!'

'Whit dae yeh mean?' (I began to feel sorry for the boabbie.)

'Whaur wiz she when yeh last saw ehr?

'She wiz goin weh ehr lad tae see him tae the last bus, an it's been gone fir ages, an eh dinna gie a buggar if she's twenty-two or ninety-two, she's gone missin, and she's meh lassie; an it's your joab tae go an get help so that weh kin find ehr!'

Just as the policeman put his notepad down, and started to say something, we were suddenly interrupted by another battering on the door and my older brother shouting:

'Is meh Mither an meh sister in there?'

The policeman quickly opened the door again, and there was my older brother, who immediately spilled out the whole tale, of how they had arrived home not too long after my mother and I had left.

He and my father had then come out to look for us, and my father was still looking, but had sent my brother up to the police box to see if we were there. Easy seen he'd been married to my mother for years!

So the policeman ushered us all out into the night with my mother saying:

'Thanks very much. Sorry fir a' the trouble. Family! It's a winder it's no me that's goin missin! Or landin up in an early grave! Sometimes Eh kid jist murder them!'

I would imagine that the policeman agreed whole-heartedly with all she was saying, but included her in that statement as well!

We started back down the road having now completely forgotten that only a short while ago we'd imagined digging my sister up from 'the foonds' where some mass murdered had slung her.

My mother starts in on my brother:

'An whit the hell possessed the three o' yeh tae jist tak aff, an no a word tae me that she widna be back in twenty meenits?'

'We'd hae missed the last tram as well if wid taen the time tae come back an tell yeh!'

'So what! Tae hell weh the last tram! Here's me thinkin she's hurt or even worse.'

At this we spied my father at the corner of the street, with a face that would've stopped King Kong in his tracks. When we got nearer he just cut straight across any conversation:

'Right! Thir's *nae* buggar missin now! So . . . Eh *don't* want tae hear the word "*missin*" any mair the night! Let's jist get hame. A' this bliddy uproar fir nothing! It could've been *me* gettin lifted if anybody hid seen iz prowlin aboot!'

Now she'd been married to him the same length of time he'd been married to her, so she *did* refrain from saying something along the lines of;

'Peety it wizna *you* that hid gone missin. Eh widna hae been nearly sae worried.'

Instead, she just put on her 'Well-Eh'm-less-than-plazed-weh-a-this-kerry-on-as-well' face! While my father had on his 'Eh-dinna-gie-a-buggar-wha's-happy-or-no' face, and my brother and I had on our 'Eh'm-no-daft-Eh'm-sayin-nothin' faces, as we all headed back home!

* * *

If I'm being honest here, and once I knew she was alright, there was a part of me that was quite happy that it was my older sister stealing the limelight for all the *wrong* reasons, for she seldom did!

It made a change from it being me!

14

WORKIN IN DUNDEE

I started in my first job when I was sixteen. I went to work with the SCWS (Scottish Cooperative Wholesale Society, known to Dundonians as the Sosh!)

There was no elastic plastic back in those days, but with the Sosh folk could 'pit thir messages on the book' and pay the bill at the end of the week.

Every time you spent money in the Sosh you were handed a wee ticket (called a check) which had a unique number. You saved up these checks and, twice a year, you were paid a dividend (yehr divi) and received some money back. Actually just like the loyalty points you get now.

The Sosh had a shop which took up the whole of the building across the road from the Wellgate Centre where Iceland is now. The office was on the first floor. The storage area was above the office and I think the top storey was flats. You must've been fit to live up there!

The main store took up the ground floor and down into the basement area. They didn't sell groceries, but they did sell almost everything else, including clothes, hardware, furniture, electrical goods and so on!

I started work in the Check Office, and my job was

to sort the duplicates of the original customer checks into order numbers, put them into the pigeon-holed boards and there were hundreds of these boards! Well, if there weren't, it seemed like that to me at the time. The checks were ferried in from all over Dundee. From square one, I knew I'd pick my spot on the bridge if I'd to spend my life doing 'checking!' However, there was the promise that I would get trained up in other office duties as well.

So, finger-licking check-counting, plus making the tea for all concerned it was. Back then the office junior's job was exactly the same as the tea laddie on a building site, only warmer and cleaner. But I bet it was much more exciting getting to learn how to use a hammer, or mix cement!

It was when I worked in the Sosh that I got my first Saturday job and I loved it! I got offered work downstairs in the big store during 'Divi' days and Saturdays.

'Divi Day' was great fun, and it had such a feel-good factor! Everyone was coming into the shop to 'get' money and then, depending on whether they could afford it or not, spend it back and earn more Divi points!

So, on 'Divi Days', you'd very few folk coming in looking for 'blood' because they weren't happy with some purchase or other, and for those who weren't happy with their amount of Divi money, then I just had to refer them to the office up the stairs.

I remember one woman who pulled about 500 checks out of her shopping bag, that she had counted up herself before she came in, and the Divi money didn't tally up with what she had, so off she stomped to the office to get them counted again! Thank the Lord I was the junior was what flashed through my mind!

On the other hand, it wasn't the first time someone

handed me a bag of sweeties because I was the one handing out the money!

And here's a thing! When I worked in the store on Saturdays, regular customers got to know your name, and if they liked you, would wait for you to serve them. Then you'd have a blether as you attended to them.

The main store had a balcony area that housed goods and the shop office. The Drapery department was the first section I worked in. They sold curtain material as well as made-up curtains. You had to measure and cut the curtains and I lived in fear that I would cut them all wrong and bang would go my Saturday job! But the woman in charge was no fool, because I never got near a pair of scissors for any big jobs!

I absolutely loved working on ladies clothing, even though at that time I thought the stuff was mainly 'Mithers an Grannies'. The Sosh had an alterations service, and after you bought your coat, for example, the dressmaker would come along to the cubicle and 'do you measurements', all in with part of the service.

Oh, that reminds me of when I would go with my grandmother when she went to buy some new clothes, and it was from her that I learned the true meaning of bargain hunting!

I recall sitting in the this particular shop after she'd chosen the coat she wanted, assured the assistant that she loved it and, since she was only five foot nothing in her stocking soles, yes it would need altering. So along came the dressmaker and pinned up the hem and the sleeves. Yes, that was perfect! Then my granny asked the assistant:

'Is the price on the ticket, the price yehr wahntin?'

Puzzled hesitation, then . . . '*Yes!*'

'Well, that's *far too dear* fir me. So Eh'm wonderin whit yeh'd tak aff o' it?'

The dressmaker looked at the assistant, and then departed back to the sanctuary of her workroom!

'But that's the price, and I can't change it!'

'Well, could yeh get the manager an see whit they hiv tae say.'

'No problem.'

Five minutes later:

'Yes, madam. Can I help?'

So we went through the whole 'that's too dear fir me' thing again with the lady who was the manager.

'Well,' says my granny, after getting another knock back, 'Eh shop here a' the time, so Eh think Eh should get a bargain when Eh'm spendin a' this money!'

The manager just looked at her! But you know what? It never failed! She always got some money off her coats! Then she would say:

'Oh! Eh! An Eh'm assumin that they alterations are fir free?'

Well, they were for her!

If we'd lived in Africa, I couldn't have been better trained if we were tracking lions!

Anyway, back to Saturdays working in the Sosh!

The store operated a Lampson system. Cash (or Provie Check which was a money guarantee from the locally well-known Provident Loan Society) was put into one of the six by three-inch round cylinders, then you opened up the tube beside the cash desk, the cylinder was sucked in with a 'SWOOSH!, flew up overhead and along the pipes and into the office. Then minutes later back it came with a 'BANG!' and landed in the basket beside the till with the receipt and the change.

Oh, then there was one particular Saturday, I was hauled

up and 'severely reprimanded' for almost destroying a whole window display!

The window dresser needed help and I was chosen to go and assist her! My job would be to hold the dummies while she dressed them and then help her stand them up.

Long ago the dummies resembled real folk; female dummies had 'sticky-oot chests' and dummies had obvious false hair stuck on top of their heads. Anyway, at the age I was, I can tell you I did *not* want to be in that window with half-naked dummies!

But there we were. The window dresser must've forgotten something she needed and departed from the window, leaving me on my own with instructions to:

'Jist hing ontae that dummy *(she was speaking to me I can assure you)* an Eh'll no be lang!'

So there I am, standing like a dummy right enough as the whole of Dundee waltzed by and then had a smile at my expense, as I stared out into space and pretended I was invisible.

Suddenly, there was this thunderous banging on the window and when I looked up, here were two girls I knew:

'Got yersel a lad?' (mouthed through the window)

'Shut up! Eh'll get intae trouble!' (mouthed back in the vain hope it would shut them up).

Nae Chance! They continued to have a laugh at my expense, so I guess I decided to join in and pretended I was dancing with the dummy.

By now a small group of spectators were beginning to gather, so I turned to get the dummy back to its place and its arm fell off! I let out a shriek, stumbled, and the dummy took off into space, crashing into everything in its path.

I dived out the window that now resembled a bomb site

and into the shop just in time to see the window dresser approaching:

'Thir's been a wee accident!'

'A wee accident?' She stepped into the window . . . I shall draw a veil over my being taken to the office and threatened with what would happened if there was ever a repeat of 'the wee accident!'

The one thing I do remember is that when we got back into the window that day, 'they twa buggars' that had caused all the trouble had vanished like a puff of dust!

* * *

When I was seventeen, I left the Sosh and went to work in the mills. That's a whole other story. I only worked in the mills for about fourteen months or so, but that really was a real life-changing experience for me!

I have never worked so hard in any other job I ever had, then or now! But the laughs I had were many. I look back on my short sojourn into that industry with a fondness and respect for the folk I met there!

My own mother worked in the mills from she was a young girl until she got married. Then she went back part-time when we were all growing up, for the extras it provided.

She was very deaf in later years and I am positive it was industrial deafness, although that was not a recognised condition back then, it was just accepted as part of the job!

It was a hard work indeed. Both my mother's thumbs were crooked by the time she retired. Her right thumb was the worst and had ridges where her scissors (mull shears) had pressed into it for all those years, and it felt like leather.

She was a reeler and a cop winder. She worked the

machine that fed the yarn onto spools for the weavers. She had to be able to work between two spools; one fed and one filled up with yarn. The ones that filled up provided spools (cops) for the weavers. So she shifted spools and tied off, and joined up ends of yarn all day long, without ever putting the machine off.

When I tell you that this machine could have between 100 and 200 spools all birling around at the same time you really had to be fast and efficient (a nabbler) to keep up with it all day!

It wasn't until I experienced working as a Weaver that I appreciated just *how* hard she did work!

I can remember I used to meet up with my mother for lunch two or three times a week at the mill canteen of the factory where she worked. I would arrive at the canteen ten minutes before she was due out; get us a table; then set about 'gettin the grub in'.

I would wait until I saw a hive of activity behind the kitchen counter, then dive down the aisle to be amongst the first in the queue, accompanied by the sound of the mid-day bummer (I wish I'd a fiver for every time in my life I'd heard one of those sirens) that released the workers for their thirty-minute lunchtime.

I'd get my food and my mother's usual; plate of soup, bread roll and a cake. Then I'd dive back and have it all set out for her as she came bustling through the door. My doing this ensured that she didn't have to join the queue that was forming, and she could sit down for practically the whole thirty minutes!

She'd dive into her seat and lift her soup spoon with a: 'Hiya! Well whit a bonny day!' Or alternatively. 'Whit a bliddy awful day!' Then . . . 'Well, how's it a' goin?'

Then we'd be off on our lunchtime conversations. Not for

the first time did I think as I saw her running through the canteen door that my money was easily earned compared to hers!

* * *

I had various jobs after the mills, including working in the Timex, a very short time with the National Cash Register (the Cash), until I eventually settled down into what would be my employment for the rest of my working life!

How many of the kids today can say they'll settle into a job for life! In my opinion, the workplace is a much more precarious place for them than it ever was for me!

I went to work for what was then Dundee Corporation (The Corpie) in the 1960s. Back then, one of the first things you had to do was go for a medical so that you could be superannuated.

It was when I went for that medical that it never ceased to amaze me that I got the job at all!

Anyway!

Off I went that morning of my medical, all duly washed and scrubbed, new bra (past the vest and liberty bodice stage), stockings (past the woollie scrape yehr legs type, thank Goad) and knickers (past the navy blue flannel with the secret pocket, what a shame)! But all this new clean underwear thing was still about maybe getting run over by that bus that just looks for folk with dirty underwear; or 'gein yehrsel a showin up at the doctors . . . or any place else for that matter!

The place where you went for your 'Corpie medical' was a two-storey building up Constitution Road. The top part was the corporation medical centre and the ground floor was the place where you went if you had a 'transmittable disease'. Back then a transmittable disease to me was the mumps or the measles.

So naturally, I ignored all the notices and went to the wrong clinic! After I'd been there for about ten minutes this guy in a white coat looks at me, puts down his clipboard and approaches:

'Excuse me, what do you want here?'

'Eh'm waitin on meh medical for Dundee Corporation.'

'Oh! Then I think they will attend to that on the upper floor.'

'Oh! Right yeh are. Thanks very much.'

With that I departed, thinking how typical it was of 'them' not to have any notices up, until I reached ground floor and saw the notices.

Later on, when someone told me where I'd been at the first clinic, the only thing I could think of was:

'Eh hope naebody Eh kent wiz in that buildin!'

But worse was yet to come!

I was by now running late for my medical and I was met at the door by this woman who was not a happy soldier:

'You are late!'

'Sorry, I got lost.'

'Right!' Sniff! 'Then hurry, let's get some tests done before you see doctor!'

And with that she marched off down the corridor and into this room.

'Please take off your shoes and coat and come over to the scales and the measure rod.'

I disrobed as instructed and over I went.

'Stand up against the measure.' She indicated the giant ruler on the wall!

'Not very tall are you?'

Well, as my mother once said to me; 'As lang as yehr

legs gae fae yehr e*** tae the grund (ground) an thir baith connected an movin, that's a' yeh hiv tae worry aboot!'

I uttered not a word. I just kept that thought to myself!

'Step on to the scales.' She indicates the scales with the huge sliding ruler across the top of them. 'You're overweight for your height.' Nothing new there then apart from *her* going up on my, 'Eh've-nae-time-fir-you' scale.

'Now we're going to do a vision test. Please take a seat and look at the poster on the opposite wall.'

She dimmed the lights, and walked over to the poster that just looked like a whole lot of tiny green dots to me. She proceeded to pick up a long school type pointer with a red metal tip. She pointed to the poster and tapped one of the tiny green dots.

'Tell me what number you see there, please?'

'What number?'

She looked at me, picked up the pointer and tried again.

'Tell me what number you see there, please?'

That did it! I'd had enough of her!

'Yeh mean tae say yeh expect me tae see a number written on a wee green dot? Is that whit yehr sayin?'

'What small green dot?' She's now looking at me as if I'd jumped down from another Planet.

'The one that yehr pointin at the now! Oh, an by the by, yeh've moved yehr pointer tae anither dot, so even if Eh did hae X-ray vision, it's a different dot!'

By now she's looking a bit rattled and my heart fills with glee . . . until . . .

'Forget all about dots and pointers for the minute! Are you telling me you do not see a number, any number at all, on the whole of the poster?'

I decided I'd better have another, closer look! And I just about had a Tartan fit!

But since I have always believed that attack is always the best means of defence at such times.

'Oh! You mean that big pink number 5 that's stuck in among a' the green dots! Well of course Eh kin see that ain! Yeh'd hae tae be blind no tae see *that!* You threw me right aff in the first place! Pointin that stick right in the middle o' a green dot!'

Now it was her turn to utter not a word. And I suppose she would have got sacked if she batted me over the head with the pointer! She sat down and began writing something on my form. Then she rose from her seat:

'Follow me, please. Now it's time to see doctor!'

And so Mrs Green-Dot and I parted company at the doctor's office. I imagined she was glad to see the back of me, but not half as glad as I was to see the back of her, for in my mind she'd now 'knackered' any chance I had of getting the job!

But lo and behold, within a couple of weeks, I got a letter from Dundee Corporation to say that I had got the job (looks like Mrs Green-Dot hadn't grassed on me, so she wasn't so bad after all), and I was to start in their new Computer Section within the month.

And that's just what I did.

* * *

Had I but known it then, my days of job-hopping were over (who can job-hop nowadays?). I was to stay; *'workin weh the Cooncil'* for the next thirty odd years, and it was to serve me well.

I always tell folk:

'Eh went tae work weh computers when the first machine Eh operated didna plug intae the wa'. Now thir pluggin intae yehr ear, an the hale world!'

And that's only in the last fifty years. With the advance in technology, workplaces are now inherently tied to computers and networking systems.

So here's to what the next fifty years will be like for the workers then. Instead of going to another building or town to look for another job, you might be going to another world!

Look out Outer Space. Here we come!

15

MEH MITHER

My mother was seventy-five years of age when Alzheimer's slithered silently through her door and began stealing her away from us.

But if it thought it could just up and away with her, then it hadn't met my mother. You're speaking about someone who had to learn at a very early age how to survive what life had to throw at her, and survive she did. She was nearly ninety before it won the battle. I remember her doctor once saying to me:

'I think one of the main reasons your mother lived so long with this condition was that she wanted to protect her family as best she could, and she just never recognised that it existed, and just adapted as best she could until it finally overtook her!'

And that just about says it all about the woman.

Although it is a ravaging illness that inflicts a whole family, she never lost her fighting spirit. This, and the ability to laugh at life even when it was dealing her a lousy hand, was something that had seen my mother through many a situation she had faced during her lifetime.

She never wasted time worrying about things that 'might

happen!' She used to say: 'Well, it might *jist* happen right enough, but us worryin oorsels tae buhts is no gonna stop it! An if it dizna happen, then think o' a the time yeh've spent worrying aboot nothing!'

She protected and guided us (her family) the very best she could, and she furnished us with some really happy memories; some of which have still kept us smiling still over the years.

* * *

I remember when I was about six years old and we still lived up the West End of the city.

Most days my mother wore a blouse (or jumper) and a skirt, which was covered with the cross-over apron that was most women's 'uniform' in my neck of the woods. She had black hair which she tucked into a bando, then stuck hairpins in the bando to keep her hair from falling out.

She was always on the go: washing; cleaning; going to the shops; going to the washie; dishing out meals; and singing (she always sang to herself) as she went about her daily business.

Then one day it was announced the Boatyard was to be having a big dance and my father had got tickets for this occasion.

Now, to my knowledge, weddings were the only 'big dos' we'd gone to before. So for weeks beforehand my mother was off to the shops looking for a new outfit. I think by the time the 'big night' arrived, we felt we were *all* going to that dance.

When you live in two rooms there's not much place to go to get ready for a night out. So we'd all to stay in the kitchen when they were getting ready 'ben the room' (the usual routine for high days and holidays when we were going somewhere special), and then they came through the room, all ready to go to their fancy night out and, to my dying day, I will never forget looking at this person that my *usual* mother had transformed into.

Sure, I'd seen her dressed up before, but this dress, this dress was something like Joan Crawford or Bette Davis would have worn in one of their films.

It was a black and pastel-coloured flowery chiffon material and had a sparkly ornament on the right-hand side of the bodice. She had black stockings and black peep toe shoes, and a wee black handbag, and her hair was all up and curly. She was better looking than any film star I'd ever seen, as she sailed forth out into the night. Funny how some memories are yours forever, eh?

* * *

Now here's the 'wringer' story. After we'd moved from the West End and had been living in Fintry for some years, the hand wringer that had replaced the big wash house spinners was getting 'past it.'

Bear in mind that, even in the 1950s, lots of houses did not have washing machines, and even if they had the room, most folk couldn't afford them at that time, and most of the women who'd moved to houses in Fintry had come from tenements and used 'The Washies' just like we did.

In our Fintry house there was a round metal boiler connected up in the kitchen, along with two big white sinks, a deep one and a shallow one, both a very long cry from the wee 10 by 8-inch black iron sink that we had in our two-roomed house up the West End. There was a raised metal plate between the two sinks for screwing a wringer on to, and these small domestic wringers were called 'Acmes'.

My mother had to wring all the washing by hand or

by feeding them through this 'toaty wee wringer', but of course she did have her very own back greenie by now (well, she only had to share it with *one* other neighbour), so she could hang out her washing more or less when she felt like it, and without any 'Washie Rammies' (public washing house disputes) over drying horses that she used to have with other women, when we lived up the West End. But you know what? I think she missed 'The Washie' for ages after we moved. I know I did!

Anyway, this particular year, my eldest sister decided that we should surprise my mother with a brand new Acme wringer for her Christmas. The one that we wanted was very expensive, because it had three settings and could wring from the smallest item up to sheets and bedcovers, which was very posh for a small wringer.

In my mind, nothing took the place of the giant mangles that had a room all to themselves in the Washie back in the old place. And even though I'd had a few 'nearly-lost-yehr-finger' escapades, I loved those mangles. You could swing on the handles when you were on your own, you could pretend it was the steering wheel on a big ship when you were turning the handle for your mother, it was a king compared to these flimsy wee new house wringers. But those days were gone forever.

My sister decided that we all start saving for the 'new Christmas wringer', and she would collect the money and then go and buy it. If memory serves we just put what we could afford, and she probably put the most as my older brother was always broke and I wasn't much better, and my two younger siblings never had much money anyway!

The wringer was duly purchased and the delivery day was a Saturday before Christmas week. We waited for the knock on the door. And it came. My mother went to the door:

'Eh've a delivery fir yeh, Missus,' says the guy pointing to this huge box with Acme Wringer emblazoned on its front.

'Eh think yeh've got the wrang hoose, son.'

He looked at his delivery list and then I think my sister must have said something like:

'No, it is fir you, Mum. It's yehr Christmas present!'

My mother was struck dumb!

We dragged the box into the kitchen and took out this magnificent piece of technology (well it was back then) and helped her get it up onto the sink. We were, of course, telling her at the same time about the fact that it had *three* settings, and how much easier it would be to 'get the manglin done now.'

My clearest memory of that day was us prattling on, when I noticed that my mother had gone silent (most unusual), and I imagined that she maybe didn't like her present. Then she spoke:

'Eh dinna think Eh've ever hid a better present than this in meh whole life!' There was another wee silence then she said: 'Right then! Whit are weh waitin fir? Let's treh it oot!'

So we did!

I recall some years later when she could afford to get one of the new twin-tub washing machines that had its very own spinner with a timer no less. I can see her yet, with her hands stuck in that twin tub, dunking and washing bits and pieces as the blade swished back and forth;

'This bliddy thing taks a day, so Eh'm jist dookin they things, an gein it a hand. Automatic! Mair like auto-buggary!' said she!

Looked like you could 'tak the wummin oot o the washie, but yeh couldna tak the washie oot o the wummin!'

* * *

Speaking of the progression of technology, my mother had absolutely no interest in how things worked, just that they did. She (like the rest of her generation) took to washing machines, hoovers, electric irons etc. like the proverbial duck to water! And why wouldn't they?

I can remember when folk had to heat their irons up on the fire, never mind just having to stick a plug into a hole in the wall. And there wasn't any need for a hoover that lifted the dust from the carpets, for there were precious few carpets and any rugs you did have, used to have to be thrown over the back greenie ropes, and whacked at with a carpet beater.

So moving forward technologically, as far as my mothers' generation of women were concerned, was a definite plus!

My father was an electrician and my mother used to drive him to distraction with her requirements for all these new electrical devices she could now afford:

'Yehr mither thinks that when she wants a new socket an plug or a new light pit in, Eh jist get a buht glue and stick the switch on the wa' an aff yeh go!'

I think this would be after my mother had said something like:

'That switch's too far doon in the coarner fir me tae get up an doon a the time when Eh'm yazin the iron or the hoover. Kid yeh no stick a switch half wey up the wa. That wid mak it a lot easier?'

On this particular Saturday morning, there was my younger brother, myself and my parents at home. My father was doing some electrical 'whatever' around the house because my mother had stated:

'They wires are comin oot o the grammie (gramophone) a' ower the place! An Eh've tae bend ahent it tae get the plug in tae dae meh hooverin. It wid be a lot better if they wires wir a' pit through the wa' an ben the room intae the dinette, an Eh kid jist shove a' the plugs intae the switches ben there.'

Our Grammie was now a mahogany coloured stand-alone piece of furniture, which had a turntable that held more than one record and had a wireless with umpteen stations. It also had a lift-up lid that had a special fixture which allowed the lid to gently slip back down, instead of just clattering with a wallop. But when my mother put on a record she just shoved the lid down anyway because, 'It wiz too bliddy slow.'

You will, of course, have noted that the Grammie was in a house that also had a dinette as well as a hoover and a washing machine! Talk about pan loafy!

So, my father had spent most of the morning sorting out Grammie wires. He came up the stairs and went round us with his usual 'electricity warnings':

'Eh'm gonna switch on the electric now tae Eh test they wires an new plugs. *Don't go near anything until Eh give yeh the okay! Dae yeh hear me?'*

My father worked in the boatyard most of his working life and witnessed first-hand what electricity could do if not treated with respect. He instilled in all of us a healthy regard for it, which I carry to this day.

So after;

'Yeh' . . . 'Yup' . . . 'Okey-Dokey . . .' from various rooms, off he went to test the Grammie.

Now my mother, who was also upstairs and up to the ears with whatever it was she was doing, must have just answered 'Yeh' . . . 'Yup' . . . 'Okey-Dokey . . .' (whichever one she was); and then totally dismissed it from her brain, for ten minutes after he'd gone back downstairs, she plugged in the hoover and switched it on; and we heard . . .

'*YAAAAAAHH!!!*' And then an almighty THUMP!

Then *silence!*

No calls of who was going to be murdered if he got them, no swearing, not anything . . . ZILCH!

We three took to our heels down the stairs, to find my father laid out at the opposite side of the room from where the plugs and sockets that he had been testing were. the grammie was shoved into the middle of the room as he had rocketed past it, and he was lying against the wall shaking his head.

'Oh! Meh Goad, John! Are yeh aright?' Shrieked my mother! (Why do people insist on that being the first words out of their mouths when the person obviously isn't?)

My father just nodded, but kept shaking his head!

'Get yehr father a drink o' wahter!'

My brother bolted from the room and back again, by which time my father was coming round. He drank the glass of water, sat up, looked at the three of us and demanded:

'WHA PIT A BLIDDY SWITCH DOON?'

My mother confessed instantly. She would've taken the blame anyway, she always did if she thought we were in real trouble with him. However, this time it was true!

'Never mind a' that jist now! It wiz me! An Eh'm sorry! But kin yeh get up an sit in the chair, an mak shair yehr a'right. An Eh'll go an mak a cup o tea!'

To our utter amazement he did just that! Not even a wee rant! However, later was yet to come, when we weren't there, and was thankfully nothing to do with us!

One conversation I never did tell him about, ever, was

that once she saw he was perfectly alright, sitting having a fag, a scone and a cup of tea, before he went back into the danger zone and my mother and I were in the kitchen on our own, she said to me:

'Did yehr father tell us that ee wiz gonna be testin they plugs?'

'Yup!'

'Well whaur wiz Eh?'

'Up the stairs as well.'

'Well . . . Ee couldna hae shouted up the stairs very loud then!'

'But Ma! *Ee came up the stairs an warned everybody!*'

'Ee niver warned me.'

'But yeh answered him! . . . *Yeh did!* . . . Yeh answered him back.'

Hesitation . . . then:

'Och ee kens fine Eh dinna listen tae half whit goes on in this hoose, so ee should've made shair Eh'd heard him! Whit a bliddy fleg! Ee could've been seriously injured. Dead even! An a this commotion ower a few wee wires gettin shifted ben the room.'

However, she was well pleased with the finished results, and for ages kept telling my father what a difference it made!

* * *

Then there's another Christmas present story which I will call the 'Winter Boots and Humongous Tights' episode.

It was about two weeks before Christmas. My younger sister and I decided to club together and get my mother these very expensive pair of boots she had been constantly admiring called 'Huskies', but when she saw the price had commented:

'Goad's sake! Eh'd need a new pair o' legs *an* a set o' real live husky doags, at the price thir askin fir they buits!'

So we said we would take her down to Potters the posh Dundee shoe shop that was somewhere in Commercial Street at that time, and treat her for her Christmas.

Do you know, my mother had a thing about *'guid'* shoes and I think it was because she couldn't always have new shoes when she was a kid, so she made up for it later on.

She always took us to Potters when we were kids because they had this machine that you stood on the wee platform and looked through the eye holes on the machine and saw your skeleton toes. I never did like that machine as I preferred my toes with the skin on, but according to 'She-who-knows-everything':

'Yeh kid see that yeh hae plenty room fir yehr taes tae grow, an they (the shoes) wid dae yeh fir a while.'

She was also known to remark in my case:

'Unless it's you, then they last aboot fehve meenits. Eh think every pavement stane in Dundee kens the marks o' you scruffin the taes oot o yehr shoes. Eh should buy you steely capped boatyaird buits!'

Actually that would've suited me just dandy, as I could've skidded and sparked my way merrily over the cobbles. But I knew that was never going to happen. They never made 'steely capped boatyaird buits' in my size! And they certainly would *not* have sold them in Potters!

But back to my sister, my mother and me, standing outside Potter's window looking at 'Her Huskies'. They were sable brown and had two zips up the front of each boot and went right up to below your knees. They were indeed a thing of beauty. My mother pointed in the window:

'Och the mair Eh think on it, that's an affy lot o' money

fir jist a pair o' buits. Eh'd get jist as much wear oot o' they ither ains that are half the price.'

'But they're no the ains that yeh really want.' *(my sister)*

'An wir treatin yeh fir yehr Christmas, so we'll get the ains yeh like the very best!' *(me)*

'Och well! If yehr shair?'

'We are! An yeh ken yeh'll jist love them! So in we go!'

I might mention here that my mother taught us that if you were doing something 'special' then you dressed for the occasion. You know the 'clean vest an knickers in case yeh get huht beh a bus' syndrome.

So on that basis, she put on new tights (with no darnings) because she would be trying on her new boots!

What we didn't know was she had bought these thick tights that were for a woman who was a size 50" across the hips and 6 foot tall, and she ignored the fact that she was about 36" across the hips and almost a stand-in for one of Snow White's crew. She never could resist a 'bargain'. Afterwards she informed us:

'Eh got they tights fir a sang, an wha kens whit yeh've got on below yehr clahes anywey? Eh've jist rolled the slack up, an thiv kept me fine an cosy.'

Cosy! When I looked at them, if she'd sewn two bits of elastic onto the waistband, she could've worn them as dungarees! Just why you have to know this will become apparent as you read on.

So now we three are sitting in the seats in Potters opposite the foot rest with its measuring equipment in a special holder on the back of the stool. We had our number card in front of us. This was a wee square card with a number which stated where you were in the queue for being served and saved any contretemps (rammies if you weren't in Potters) about queue jumping.

The assistant, who was a pleasant young guy, dressed neatly in a suit and tie, had a long, bone shoehorn attached with a thin chain to his belt:

'Good morning, Ladies. May I help you?'

'We'd like to look at the Huskie twin zipped boots for my mother. Size 3.'

'Certainly Madam!'

He pushed over the footstool in front of my mother:

'Can I take your foot measurements, Madam?'

'Right yeh are, son.'

Do you know he could've been the President of America and he would've still been 'son' to my mother! Anyway, 'son' proceeded to help my mother take off her old boots, to reveal her . . . 'Nora Batty tights' that were concertinaed down to her ankles.

The assistant politely ignored this (of course), as he measured her feet and popped off to get her 'Huskies'!'

'Ma, yeh'll hae tae puhl up yehr tights, thir a' banjoed doon at yehr ankles.'

(*Me between my teeth*)

'Oh! Right yeh are.' Pull-drag-shuffle-squirm (*my mother*).

'Here we are! These are really lovely boots, which will see you through any kind of weather!' (*the assistant*).

Whizz! Whizz! Down went the zips on the new boots.

'Right foot first please, Madam.'

So, 'Madam' donned her new fancy boots and paraded up and down the carpet to the full-length mirror, admiring herself like she was the Duchess of Windsor, accompanied by all three of us telling her how well they suited her, and was she comfortable in them? My sister and I were well pleased that she looked so happy. It would be money well spent!

'Oh! Thir absolutely marvellous. Thir that cosy; an Eh feel like Eh'm wahkin on air.'

'Right then! That's settled! We'll have them.' *(my sister)*

'May I help you take them off, Madam?''

'Eh right yeh are, son,' says she, offering a boot for unzipping.

But unbeknown to us, one of toes of her tights had stuck in the fur that went right down into the toe of boot, and when the shop assistant pulled, the leg on her tights just kept on getting longer . . . and longer and . . . just longer still!

To this day, I can see this guy's face as he kept trying to ease the boot discreetly from her foot, without letting on he was taking the tights with it, and desperately trying to remember what they'd told him in training that would cover this kind of caper!

But my mother, as ever, came to his 'rescue':

'Hing on son! Eh'll jist grab a handfuhl at the tap o they tights, at meh wehst, an ane o them *(that would be us)* kin puhl the tae o meh tights fae the buit.'

'Son' was trying to 'hing on' alright, but it was to his dignity, as the customers round about us watched as he went backwards with the huge roll of black nylon chewing gum on the end of the fancy Huskie boot!

I leaned over swiftly and wheeched the offending tight out of the boot and it just hung there like a huge piece of black scrunchy knicker elastic, dangling from the end of my mothers' foot. Undaunted she stood up!

'Wait a meenit! Eh'll jist stand up an puhl it a' back intae place.'

And that's exactly what she did! In the middle of Potters no less!

I can remember my sister and I about bursting a gasket laughing when we got out the shop. We still do when we speak about it and I'm sure she'll be smiling away as she reads this!

My mother's take on it:

'Oh! they buits are jist the bees knees! Yeh shouldna hae spent a' that much money! But Eh love them tae buhts! Eh canna wait till Eh treh them oot! . . . Whit are you twa laughin at?'

We told her.

'Whit dae yeh mean, the laddie aboot died o' embarrassment? Whit embarrassment? He'd jist selt a pair o buits that cost a sma fortune, so ee should be well happy! An eez helluva easy embarrassed if seein a pair o tights diz it!'

* * *

Then, there was the day when she had just finished her part-time work at the mill and came out the mill gate to find a blizzard blowing.

So she got herself and her two bags of shopping ('messages' to us) up to the bus stop, got on a bus, only to reach the terminus at Maryfield to be informed by the bus conductor that the bus,'Couldna get doon the Forfar Road brae, an they'd a' hae tae get aff an walk!'

So, ejected from the bus, she knotted her head square tightly round her head and joined her fellow pilgrims in their trek home. She had on an old pair of boots and the soles weren't quite gripping, and she was slipping all over the place. So she went up the driveway of one of the houses that were on the Forfar Road, and took out a spare scarf that she had in her message bag, which was now to come in handy for one of her 'yaze whit yeh hiv an yeh'll niver wahnt' situations.

Taking out her wee reeler's knife, she cut the scarf in two, wound and then tied both bits round her boots, stood up and tested the ground. Eureka! It worked! So she re-knotted her head square and stepped once more into the blizzard to continue down the road for home. All was going well until she hit a real icy patch, skidded, took off and landed in a heap. A young guy came to her aid immediately:

'Are yeh aright, Missus? Yeh took aff there like yeh'd been shot fae a cannon!'

'Eh! . . . Eh'm fine, son. . . . Help iz up!'

He leaned over and spotted her bound feet.

'Meh Goad, Missus. Whit's that yeh've on yehr feet? Yeh'll freeze tae death!' Look, let me help yeh.'

With that he proceeds to go into his coat pocket and get his wallet and it dawned on my mother:

'Oh no, son! Eh've got meh buits on below the buhts o' scarf! They're jist tae keep iz fae slippin. But if yeh *really* wahnt tae help yeh could tak a bag.'

So he did, and they came home together. When she was relating this story she laughed as she recalled the look on his face:

'Ee must've thought Eh wiz a refugee o some kind. An here's me jist comin hame fae meh work. But wizn't that kind o' him that ee wiz maybe gonna offer me some money. See whit dae Eh tell yeh! The world's fuhl o guid fowk!'

She held that firm belief to the day she died.

* * *

I could fill a book with anecdotes about my mother and still have some left over.

If you asked most of the folk who knew her, and who lived beside us in Fintry, to describe my mother, I think they would say something like:

'Och! Eh! Your mither's the wee wummin weh the twa bags o' grub, an the twa half loafs below ehr erms, that's aye runnin.'

The last 'Mither' anecdote I would like to share with

you happened when my mother was a pensioner in her seventies and attended a pensioners club where she lived.

As usual, she involved herself, and was on some committee or other in the club and must have been in charge of ordering pies and bridies from the local butcher once or twice a week, for those who wanted them to take home for their tea. And, as she informed me when I was up at her house eating one of those delicacies:

'Eez a brah butcher, an geez us a bargain o the pehs an bridies, an the laddie brings them tae the clubbie, so weh dinna even hae tae gae tae the shop. Is that no affy good o' him?'

One teatime when I visited on a 'peh-or-bridie-day', I just got in the door when she pounced with the story:

'The pehs an bridies are in the oven, but wait'll yeh hear whit happened the day up at the clubbie!'

I was all ears as she burst forth with the saga.

'Eh wrote oot the list fir the butcher the day, an thir wiz a lot o the members wahntin pehs an bridies, so Eh wizzna surprised when the laddie fae the butcher appeared at the door weh a brahed (bread) board, until Eh looked at the number o' bridies, and meh Goad, they wid've fed the hale o' the Black Watch, niver mind a handfuhl o' pensioners. Eh looked at the butcher's laddie:

"Wha on earth's a' they bridies fir?"
"That's whit yeh ordered, it's on yehr list."
"Niver in yehr Nellie! Gie me a look at the list." '

The young guy handed her the paper and listed on it was:

14 pies
10 bridies
6 0 bridies.

My mother held her hands up in the air even as she related the tale to me:

'Eh spotted eez mistake right away!' (Take note it's the butcher's laddie's fault).

'Son that's no *sixty*. Dae yeh no see the space in between the numbers? An anywey whit wid Eh dae askin ten bridies on ae line, an then the line below it askin anither sixty?

'That's six, space 'O'! An the 'O' is fir . . . ingin.

'How on earth dae yeh think us pensioners could eat a' they bridies? Yeh'll jist hae tae tak maist o' them back. Or yeh kin ask the butcher if ee wahnt's us tae tak them aff eez hands on the cheap!'

And with that she up and paid him for sixteen bridies and fourteen pies and saw him off the premises.

If memory serves me, I think the butcher did came back and offer them at a reduced price, rather than bin them I would imagine, and sold some of his extra bridies to them. So they all got a bargain, apart from the butcher that is!

To those of you who still haven't quite got it about the bridie mistake, here's a request whilst in a famous Dundee pie shop in Castle Street (not with us any more), that should make everything crystal clear:

'Eh'll hae a peh, a plehn bridie, an an ingin ane ana!'

* * *

Which reminds me of the Dundee man I heard about, who went into a shop that sold newspapers as well as pies and bridies, and although I can't swear to the truth of this wee story, I love it!

English first:

'Can I have five meat pies, four plain steak pasties, and could I have one steak and onion pastie as well? And I'll have an *Evening Telegraph* also'.

(The *Evening Telegraph* is our local newspaper known to Dundonians one and all as *The Tullie).*

In Dundaneeze, that very cleverly translates to:

'Eh'll hae fehve pehs, fower plehn bridies, an an ingin ane ana. An Eh'll tak a Tullie tae.'

Concise, to the point and much more colourful, don't you think?

* * *

Now where was I?

Ah yes, my mother!

What always amazed (and entertained) me about my mother was how she just kept going. She enjoyed her life to the full for as long as she could. She solved all problems in her own particular fashion and moved on, be it pehs or predicaments, bridies or blizzards, tornadoes or Tullies!

And keep on going she did, until she could no longer run, then she just slowed to a walk. She used to say to me as she got older, 'Eh'm keepin on the move, fir they canna hit a movin target,' which I much preferred to her other laughing comment on getting old:

'When yeh stop readin the deaths in *the Tullie*, yeh ken yehr headin fir the front pew, an it's nae bliddy joke!'

I'm at the age myself now where I'm beginning to understand exactly what she meant. So if you see a 'wee wummin runnin fuhl tilt roond the toon', chances are it'll be me trying to keep on go and dodge the arrows heading for the target!

My mother died just a few months away from her ninetieth birthday. My world changed dramatically and forever, and she left a massive void for us all to fill.

She was a hard act to follow, although she would've wondered what the hell I was speaking about if she could have read this.

She never had much formal education at all, but she sure had a Class A diploma from the school of life! She was an astute, strong woman. She was kind, street-wise, she had a great sense of humour *and* she was one of the finest humanitarians I have ever met . . . then and now! I was privileged to have had her as a mother!

I filled the void as she once told me she had to do, when she lost folk that she loved:

'Yeh've jist tae paper ower the cracks. Pit ae fuht in front o the ither, ae day at a time, an jist dae yehr best, until yehr auld normal fades, an yehr new normal kicks in.

'Fir whit else kin yeh dae?'

So that's just what I had to do:

'Fir whit else *could* Eh dae?'

But you know what? Given time, into the void poured all these memories of her that I hold close in my heart, to this very day!

16

MEH FATHER

My father would have been 100 years old this year. I often wonder what he would have thought of what's happened to us (the working classes) since he died, which was thirty-five years ago. I bet he's shaking his head in disbelief at the state of some of the political scenarios nowadays. Actually, so am I!

Where I live I can see right across the River Tay to Fife. From my window I can see this wee bridge that spans the railway lines, and as I look across to the sheds that stand sentinel along the waterfront now, in my mind's eye I can see the Caledon Shipyard of my childhood, with all its big cranes and the boats that were half-built or in for repair, and the huge wrought iron gates with the company name gilded on them.

It was through this very gate or ('ower the wa at knockin aff time') that the men who worked in 'The Yaird' spewed forth every night, up the brae and onto the steps, or over the bridge and up onto the road, to pile into the boatyard buses that were all lined up waiting to take the workers back to the nearest point to where they lived.

I recall very clearly standing at the terminus bus stop in Fintry with my father, as he collected signatures to say there was now enough folk living in Fintry to warrant a 'Boatyaird' bus! These buses were duplicates (duppies) and they ran in tandem with the usual bus service that was provided in your area.

Sometimes, when I look out the window, it's like looking at an invisible graveyard, for there are no monuments to the skill and work that took place in that shipyard: no tribute to the men or the ships they built there; not a whisper of all the struggles that went on for better wages and conditions; not even a wee plaque as far as I can see!

My father was a 'sparkie (electrician) weh the Yaird' when it was very much alive, and the stories with which he would regale us were many, hilarious and far too outrageous *not* to be true!

I can see him in my child's mind's eye, as he lifts his haversack with his 'pieces', his milk bottle, wee bags of tea and sugar to last him the day, and last, but by no means least, his 'tea can', which was usually an old syrup tin or the like. He'd have bored two holes in the sides and threaded wire through the can for lifting it from the fire. I can remember him blackening it with soot to 'tak the newness aff it' before he took a new tea can to work for the first time. Then he'd don his 'workin bunnet' and off he'd go!

Now, to speak of my father and not mention his 'bunnet' (flat cap) would be to ignore an integral part of him, because from the day I remember him he wore a bunnet to his work, and at the weekend too if it was cold!

Working bunnets and dress bunnets were always kept separate! But it was the working bunnet that fascinated me, for it could do so many other things other than keep your head warm!

Bunnets saved you from getting burnt on the head by a falling red hot rivet that some riveter, who was working overhead in the ship, accidently (or not so accidently) dropped. If it did burn your bunnet, I would imagine you would request that the fellow be more careful in the future, or words to that effect!

Bunnets saved you from the sparks from the welders' arcs, as they worked overhead. When I think about it now, my father's bunnet was always peppered with small burn holes.

Bunnets could be used to lift your tea can from the fire, wipe the bench (or more likely the floor) before you sat down. You could stick your bunnet over your face if you wanted to have forty winks at lunchtime. You could keep any letters (or your horsie-lines if you were that way inclined) that were handed to you, safe under your bunnet until you got home, unless it was 'yehr cairds', in which case I bet you felt like thumping the guy who delivered it and sticking it under his bunnet!

But, as far as my father was concerned, wearing a *new* bunnet to his work was a big no-no. He'd only wear an old bunnet (preferably frayed) that was nearly done because:

'Eh'm no wantin every daft buggar in the Yaird that sees the split new bunnet as their ain personal bulls-eye target, an decidin that thir mission fir the day is tae drap anythin at a' on meh heid!'

So he would rub soot from the chimney all over the old bunnet, then shake it off and rub what was left in. He'd scrunch it up until it looked like 'a half pund o' auld mince', then the bunnet was ready to start work in the Yaird!

To the day he died, if a bunnet wasn't on his head, then you could bet it would be in his pocket or on the back seat of his car!

* * *

Deciding to dedicate a chapter each to my mother and father has made me stop and think! It's really strange isn't it, what a lottery life is?

Here's the real scary bit though (scarier than any horror picture), you have absolutely no choice in the selection of parents. We are, each and every one of us on this planet, accidents of birth!

You wouldn't even buy a new coat without trying it on first to see if it fitted you and you looked good in it, and here you are getting fitted out with 'a life' before you can even walk or talk, never mind get to interview whoever gets to take care of you for the very first x amount of years of your life!

When you're a kid your folks are just your folks. I have always believed that if you're lucky, you're born somewhere half decent, and if you're not so lucky, then that can steer your course in life as well.

And it doesn't *all* have to be about money! Sure that helps when your part of the world is officially about how much you've got financially, so having plenty money ensures your comfort and certain privileges in your society. But that's about all it does as far as I can see.

My own experiences have taught me that *who* you are as an adult is, most of the time, down to the folk that have been looking after you at the start of Round One!

So although I'd never ever claim perfection in my family, ('And how no?' That's my mother speaking now) I think my stars were just fine when it was decided I should join my household!

Writing about my mother was easier than writing about my father. Her escapades were so many that I had to select the ones I loved the best. Life in her opinion should be looked straight in the eye, and then *ignored as much as possible!*

A Mother quote on some impending event or crisis:

'Forget it . . . it's no happened yet! An as lang as it's no terminal, life's far too serious fir anybody tae tak it a' in earnest anyway!'

Or for lesser crisis:

'It's far fae yehr e***, so yeh'll no hae tae sit on it!'

(The clue to what e*** means is in the 'sit on it' bit),

A Father quote on the same impending event or crisis:

'Right, go ower athin agen! At the moment thir's nothin tae be done, but yeh hiv tae think whit wey tae deal weh it; an then yehr armed nae matter whit happens!'

Or for lesser crisis:

'If that's a yeh hiv tae worry aboot, then awa an help somebody that's got a real worry!'

My father was a whole other ball game from my mother! He liked a laugh as well as the next person. And yes life should also be looked straight in the eye and then *dealt with immediately!*

* * *

To write anything about my father at all would have to include his politics, for they were a huge part of who he was. My father was involved politically from the age of nineteen when he joined the Communist party! He remained a member all his life.

He was a Shop Steward or on shop steward committees in most of the places he worked in. He was involved with his Union, the ETU, all his working life, and from the day I can remember him, he was involved one way or another with 'fightin the cause' as it used to be known. If he wasn't away delivering pamphlets, he was away delivering the *Daily Worker,* or he'd be away to some rally, protest march or meeting.

In later life, he had many tales to tell about the struggles that went on, and I recall now this story he used to tell me about when he was in his early twenties and had not long started working in the Caledon. They were campaigning for paid holidays in the Yaird, and not just a 'lock out'. 'Lock out' meant you were off for the week to allow maintenance and safety checks, but you got no wages!

My father was sitting one 'piece time' speaking to this man who'd spent all his life working on ships, and he was trying to persuade the man that if they stuck together then they could all have a week off *and* get paid as well, but the man had told him it was just a pipe dream.

'But,' said my Dad, years later, when he told me the story, (yet again), 'Eh've lived lang tae see the proof o' what stickin thegither can dae! Eh see a' meh femly in joabs that are superannuated and getting at least eight weeks holidays weh wages, so anything's possible if yeh remember wha's side yehr on!

'An if yeh forget that, then they'll jist tak it a' back.'

* * *

My mother (the philosopher, who was also a socialist) brought us up on her own for a good deal of the time, and 'put up' with his political involvements because in her words:

'Well that's yehr father. It alwiz wiz! An ee could be dain a lot worse things than trehin tae better wir lot.'

* * *

But of course there was a whole other side of him apart from his politics!

Once when I was a kid, I pointed to this scar that he had on the side of his neck (from some small operation I think) and asked him what it was.

'Oh! That! Eh got that when Eh wiz fightin the Zulu oot in Africa durin the Boer War, an ane o' them very nearly killed me beh throwin eez spear at iz, an jist missin beh an inch!'

'Did yeh nearly kill him back?'

'Na that wid've been really wrang. So Eh jist telt him no tae dae it agen!'

That somehow didn't tie in for me with the instructions I always received from him when some kid was trying to bully me:

'Get back oot there an hit them back, niver mind how big they are, jist get stuck in!'

Therefore, I would have much preferred if he'd 'mallied' that Zulu! That would have made a much better ending to the story. However, I still used to bring my pals in to see his battle scar . . . until I knew better.

In the main, when we were all younger, my mother's was the most spoken, and most demonstrated, love and pride, and his was mostly unspoken, but never did I doubt that it was there. We all knew that he would do anything in his power for any one of us, and he was always there on your side when he was needed!

The one thing he *did* put up with for all his life; sometimes with good grace (or *not*, as I can testify to) was half the escapades concerning my mother.

* * *

In later years, when we had all flown the nest and they could afford it, they bought a car, and at long last my mother didn't have to be humphing 'the messages'.

The car provided the two of them with a freedom they had never experienced before.

My father loved the open countryside and he was in

his element driving his car and 'gain awa up the glens' or someplace like that, after the working week was over.

They would take off on a Sunday morning early. In the boot of the car would be the picnic table and chairs, the wee stove he made (which my mother nearly blew up, and very nearly burnt us all to bits, one Sunday at the beach), the frying pan and the bacon and eggs, and the goodies for the cup o' tea, the Sunday papers, and the promise of a fish supper on the road home. So off they'd go to freedom and peace and quiet!

I don't think my mother was as keen on this 'my heart is in the Highlands' stuff as he was.

My young sister and her family were living in Glasgow by this time, and my mother much preferred going through to visit her and her family for the weekend, where my mother could get to spoil her grandkids, and she and my sister could go to the shops and look for all the bargains in Glasgow.

Some of my mother's comments on her Sundays up the glens:

- 'Meh Goad! Yehr father loves up they glens! Eez aye gain on about the tranquillity, and the peace an quiet!'
- 'Quiet? Thir's they sheep that jist fa'aboot whaur the like! Thir's as many o' them oot on the roads jist waitin on gettin bashed weh a car! An a' they tractors a 'gutterin' up the roads weh drehvin in an oot the fields efter thiv dug them a' up!'
- 'An they coos; well 'nuff said aboot their "messages" when yeh're howkin ower the field fir a spot tae hae yehr picnic! An the fehve million birds twitterin awa!'
- 'An as fir they airplanes that fleg the livin' 'daylights oot o' yeh as they whizz past yeh that low they kid read the Sunday papers ower yehr shither (shoulder)!'

- 'QUIET . . .? It's like the bliddy High Street on a Saturday night. Ach! Anywey! If it keeps him happy on a Sunday, then Eh suppose that's aright then! An right enough yehr grub and yehr biley-up oot in the open tastes smashin!'

Here's this woman who has worked in the deafening noise of the mills all her working life complaining about countryside noises!

Also, I think she completely missed the point that it was 'people' (including us as well, I would imagine) that he wanted rid of on his day off!

Anyway, having now found this car-freedom they decided they would motor up North for two weeks' holiday, and were to be stopping at wee undiscovered places and just taking their time, and doing what they wanted for a whole two weeks.

My mother was to be the navigator! I smiled at that then, as I smile now (although I get my sense of direction from her so I've no room to smile at anybody).

Anyway, before they left for the far-off North my father went over the maps with her, and she said 'right yeh are' in the correct places and never gave them more than a passing glance. She said to me when he wasn't around:

'Meh Goad! Yeh'd think weh wir goin on an expedition tae the Sahara! Wir only goin up the road!'

I, of course, held wise council (myself) and waved them goodbye as they set off and 'went up the road.'

When they arrived back home, and after the usual 'whit wiz the weather like, and whit did yeh get up tae' questions, my mother said to my father:

'Well tell ehr aboot the Kiltie. Yeh ken yehr burstin tae!'

'Okay!' says he. 'Well, yehr Mither wiz daen ehr "Pioneer in the Wilderness act" weh the map, an weh wirna sure o' whaur weh wir. So accordin tae her, weh hid tae go through this village called 'Incliss' tae get back tae the main roads, an then tak it fae there!

'In the middle o' the village wiz ane o' they war memorials weh a kiltie standin on the tap o' it, an she says; "Go right here, past that Kiltie", sticking ehr hand in front o' meh face as usual, "an doon that road." So aff weh goes, drehves on fir aboot an hour and lands back up at the same village weh the Kiltie.

'"Hing on," says she. "Wiv taen the wrang road. Weh maybe should've tain the ither turnin. Lets treh takin that road." So aff weh goes agen! An yes yeh've guessed it, aboot an hour later. Back tae Kiltie Land.

'"Let *me* hae a look," says I, takin the map fae ehr. "Whit village are yeh lookin at?"

'"That village," says she, pointin tae a road on the map that had "UNCLASS" written on it (as in unclassified)!

'Wid been goin roond in circles, roond a' they wee 'B' roads that led strecht back tae that bliddy Kiltie!'

At this my mother took up the cudgel!

'Eh but whit yehr no sayin is that weh wir in the middle o' the country, in the dark, and Eh wiz trehin tae read that wee writin weh a torch. How the hell dae yeh tell ae load o' fields fae anither ane?

'An yeh'll notice you niver took a shot o' trehen tae read the map! How did you no realise that 'Incliss' meant 'unclassified eh? An if yeh knew weh wir lost, yeh should've stopped an read the map yersel! You're the ane that likes roamin roond the country an jist landin up whaur the fancy taks us.'

Now it's back over to him:

'Eh! But no when Eh spend the whole bliddy night landin back up at some Kiltie!'

Fair enough! So the holiday went fine then! I knew when sitting on the sidelines was a good idea!

* * *

Do you know, my mother and father were like chalk and cheese. To anyone looking on, she was the chatty, happy one, and he was the serious, responsible one. But they were both strong personalities in their own way.

Anyway, they were married for forty-seven years, without a murder being committed, so something must've worked!

My father was the one who taught me that I should never defer to anyone simply because of the status they have, and that each person should *earn* the respect that is due to them.

He was the one who taught me that education, education, education of any kind, opens the doors that allow you more life choices.

He was the one that taught me that the one who *usually* limits you in what you do in life, the rules you live by, and who you become . . . is *you*.

He once said to me:

If a 100 fowk are dain wrang in *your* opinion, an you join in jist fir the sake o' no bein the only ane sayin it's wrang, yeh hivna made it right! Yeh've only made it 101 fowk dain wrang as far as you're concerned!

So wir eh no better stickin tae yehr guns in the first place.

* * *

In later years, when they were both in their late fifties or sixties, my mother used to go to the bingo with her pals on a Tuesday night. I lived near the town and so my father started coming up to visit me after he'd dropped her off at the bingo and having a blether with me, rather than trail all the way back to Mill-o-Mains (where they now lived, which is next door to Fintry) and then having to come out again later on to pick her up and take her home.

I look back on these visits now as 'the twa pancakes in jam, an three cups o' tea, Tuesdays' for that's always what he used to have as we sat and blethered. It was just like when I got him to myself as we walked along the road on Saturday morning, to the library in Blackness Avenue, up the West End of Dundee, when I was a kid! But now I could really join in the conversation. We spoke about family things, my work and, of course, politics! We had a great time ripping up all the right-wing politicians of the day, and thoroughly enjoyed setting the world to rights!

We would speak about 'the kids' (his grandchildren and my nieces and nephews, of course). Like any other Granda he spoiled them!

When I asked him once what he'd done with the 'rule book' that he used to bring us all up with, he just smiled and said:

'Well, Eh dinna hae tae write rule books fir meh grand-children. That's thir ain mither an father's joabs! Eh kin jist enjoy them, an better still, Eh hand them back fir somebody else tae dae a' the hard bits!'

I was a bit taken aback the first time he said that to me. I thought:

'Geezo! Eh niver in meh puff imagined that bein the Bringer o' Rules an Justice wiz any bahther tae him at a'!'

When the Tuesday visit was over, he'd look at his watch, then stick on 'eez bunnet' with a:

'Well, Eh'd better awa an pick up yehr mither, an hear how she jist *niver* became rich beh *almost* winnin a' they gemes at the bingo!'

Then he'd depart out the door with his usual:

'Right! Eh'm aff! Pick yeh up on Seturday at 12 o'clock as usual tae tak you an ehr ladyship intae the toon. Be ready when eh ring the bell! The fitba/tennis *(whatever Saturday sport was on in the afternoon)* is on, an eh'm no missin the start o' the match so Eh kin gie you a lift inta the toon!' *(Fair enough, Father).*

And how I missed those Tuesday visits when they came to an end!

* * *

My father died when he was just over sixty-five years of age. He only got twenty-four weeks retirement after working since the age of seventeen.

If there is somewhere else after we've all done our stint here, then he's sure had a big surprise, but if it's the place that folk crack it up to be, then I'm also just as sure that they've let him in!

My mother, when it was her turn, would have appeared at 'The Gates' already seeking out her old pals and picking the street she wanted to live in for all eternity.

At this moment in time, I can just picture her running all over the place, boring the pants off the neighbours with her 'modest' comments of:

'Meh lassie's written *anither* book! Oh eh, she'd written ain *afore* this as well! Is that no *marvellous!* When Eh think aboot it . . . we yazed tae gae alang the road *tae* the library an now, we're a' *in* the library! Is that no jist the bees knees?'

I hope nobody has the audacity to disagree with her. Getting your wings clipped would take on a whole new dimension for them!

My father, on the other hand, is just saying; if folk ask him about it:'Yeh! That's right enough; she's written a couple o' books so Eh believe! An why not? Mair power tae ehr elbow! Good for her!'

But, you know what?

I know exactly what he's thinking!

17

ACH, EH'VE RUN OOT O' PAGES

My sincere hope is that you feel (to some extent) the same as me about this chapter's heading. If you do, then I'll have done a half decent job.

Not so long ago I had my seventieth birthday. Some of my cards had the numbers printed on them and I kept thinking:

'Any meenit now the wummin in meh street that hiz a birthday the same time as me, is gonna chap that door, an ask fir ehr birthday cairds back!' But she didn't; so I just had to keep them!

In my head, I still 'see me' (most of the time) in my favourite black patent shoes and fancy wee white socks with the flowers on the sides, or in my 3½-inch sling-back high heels, dancing along the cracks in the pavement! The only difference nowadays is instead of a rumba I sometimes have to do a quick step or a waltz!

My mother's take on getting older was; 'It's a helluva lot better than the alternative.'

Well, Eh canna argie weh that, Mither.

Mark Twain once said: 'Age is just a question of mind over matter, and if you *don't* mind, then it *won't* matter!'

An, Eh canna argie weh that either!

I've had such great time writing about my memories. It's allowed me, yet again (through my trusty computer keyboard), to visit with my family and friends, some who are not here physically anymore, and revisit 'the auld days' with them.

But more importantly, as I roamed through my mind, setting down the pages for this book, it has let me be any age I *want* to be, all over again.

I smiled all the way through the chapter about my Mother's antics, and I had a few 'pancake an cup o' tea' conversations (in my head) with my father.

It's provided a talking point for my family and friends, even those who were too young to remember any of it. They've all been gracious enough to let me to babble on about 'meh book', and they've offered their own take on how different (or not so different) things are now.

And you know what I think? Some things change and some things just turn over and over again with each generation.

If you're over a certain age, you'll remember most of the escapades we all got up to 'back then'. I firmly believe that no matter where you live (for we're all the same under our skin), and once you've cracked the code that is called 'dialect', then I'm sure you got up to exactly the same antics (if not all) that I did, way back 'afore the horse an kert (cart)'.

* * *

Now, I'm going to sound like an advert for Dundee again, but that's always been alright by me!

Not so long ago, I visited the newly refurbished museum when it re-opened and it is magnificent! Very well done indeed to all concerned, you should all be very proud of yourselves!

It was great to see so many families there on re-opening day. There's a large open room for arts and crafts especially for the kids. I'd have thought I was in heaven if they'd had that when I was young!

But I got a huge surprise that day from one of my nieces and her family for my birthday in the form of an early birth-day present. They arranged for my name to be included, as a benefactor, on the huge glass plates that hang on the wall in the atrium on the ground floor.

As I stood there looking at my name I thought:

'Well wha'd hae thought when Eh wiz runnin roond the auld museum lookin fir meh very favourite big broon Russian bear so ee could scare iz tae buhts weh eez big pointy clazz (claws), an then runnin intae the art gallery weh its posh roond velvet settees tae look at meh very favourite picture o' they twa fancy ladies in thir fancy floaty frocks, that Eh'd be up on the wa' mehsel ae day!'

* * *

Who'd have thought it?

That anecdote leads me quite nicely to what I have always believed; the young care every bit as much now as we ever did when we were their age. Life is harder for them in many more ways, than it ever was for me.

I never had the unending pressures of a commercially functioning world where money is King, therefore, where does the lack of it leave you?

Long ago, everybody in my world was in the same boat. It might have not been a posh boat, the waters were some-times really rough, and I sure as hell am glad I wasn't left back there paddling away forever more, but it was *'oor boat'* and we knew the whole crew!

Now, many of the young have to survive by paddling their *own* canoe and are at the mercy of all the bigger boats!

But I'm absolutely certain they'll keep afloat. We did, didn't we?

So, in today's uncertain times, doesn't it make you feel better to know that some things are everlasting? It does me!

Anyway, here I am at the end of another literary adventure and who knows where the next road (literary or otherwise) will lead me.

I might just take up absailing, or go and see the gorillas in the rainforests of Africa, or just look up at the sky or watch the grass grow instead!

One thing is for sure! I intend to keep on dancing over the cracks in the pavements for as long as I can!

Or I might just click my heels and do a Dorothy and land up in Oz!

Hey! That soonds like a guid idea!

Geez they rade sparkly shoes 'tull Eh get them a' polished up, so that Eh'm ready fir the aff.